ANXIETY

ANXIETY

A PHILOSOPHICAL GUIDE

SAMIR CHOPRA

PRINCETON UNIVERSITY PRESS

PRINCETON & OXFORD

Copyright © 2024 by Princeton University Press

Princeton University Press is committed to the protection of copyright and the intellectual property our authors entrust to us. Copyright promotes the progress and integrity of knowledge created by humans. By engaging with an authorized copy of this work, you are supporting creators and the global exchange of ideas. As this work is protected by copyright, any reproduction or distribution of it in any form for any purpose requires permission; permission requests should be sent to permissions@press.princeton.edu. Ingestion of any IP for any AI purposes is strictly prohibited.

Published by Princeton University Press
41 William Street, Princeton, New Jersey 08540
99 Banbury Road, Oxford OX2 6JX

press.princeton.edu

GPSR Authorized Representative: Easy Access System Europe - Mustamäe tee 50, 10621 Tallinn, Estonia, gpsr.requests@easproject.com

All Rights Reserved

First paperback printing, 2025
Paperback ISBN 9780691246147
Cloth ISBN 9780691210674
ISBN (e-book) 9780691246130
Library of Congress Control Number: 2023036935

British Library Cataloging-in-Publication Data is available

Editorial: Rob Tempio and Chloe Coy
Production Editorial: Jaden Young
Text and Jacket/Cover Design: Karl Spurzem
Production: Erin Suydam
Publicity: Alyssa Sanford and Carmen Jimenez
Copyeditor: Kathleen Kageff

This book has been composed in Arno Pro with Franklin Gothic Std

For Noor and Ayana, who delivered me from fear

All existence makes me nervous.

> KIERKEGAARD

O the mind, mind has mountains; cliffs of fall
Frightful, sheer, no-man-fathomed.

> GERARD MANLEY HOPKINS

He hath heart who knoweth fear but vanquisheth it; who seeth the abyss, but with pride. He who seeth the abyss but with eagle's eyes—he who with eagle's talons graspeth the abyss: he hath courage.

> NIETZSCHE

The ultimate task of therapy ... is to help patients reconstrue that which they cannot alter.

> IRVIN YALOM

CONTENTS

Acknowledgments	xi
Our Age(s) of Anxiety	1
Becoming and Being Anxious	16
The Anxieties of Existence	35
Free to Be Anxious	53
The Death of Certainty	60
Faith, Spiritual Deliverance, and The Concept of Anxiety	71
The Courage to Be	85
The Uncanny Mood of Anxiety	94
Repression, Conflict, Memorable Trauma	108
Anxiety and the Social	124
Living with Anxiety	143
Notes	165
Bibliography	175
Index	181

ACKNOWLEDGMENTS

Without whom, not: Noor Alam, Sumbul Alam, Bradley Armour-Garb, Will Braun, Justin Caouette, Akul Chopra, Ashutosh Chandra Chopra, Ayana Prabha Chopra, Prabha Chopra, Pramod Chandra Chopra, Ritu Chopra, Skye Cleary, Chloe Coy, Japhy Dhungana, Sam Dresser, Christian Fox, Nick Gibson, Ken Haller, Martin Harvey, John Hauck, Lynn Hill, Hermione Hoby, Emma Hulme, Rob Israel, Kartik Jaggi, Kathleen Kageff, Marilyn Komisar, Ray Kozma, Ben Kunkel, Robert LeClair, Jacob Leivent, Chris Letheby, David Makowski, Gordon Marino, Eric Martin, James Martin, Brad Mering, Bentley Newton, Rohit Parikh, Nash Redmond, David Rondel, Luis Ruiz, Sunayna Sabharwal, Sanjay Sen, Robert Smith, Justin Steinberg, John Tambornino, Matt Thomas, Priya Tuli, David Turnbull, and Bill Wright; the Seize the Moment Podcast, the Ant and the Grasshopper Podcast, and the Denver Crux Podcast; the Institute for Contemporary Psychotherapy; my fellow philosophical counselors; those who placed faith and trust in my counseling, shared a rope with me, or gave me a belay. I owe particular thanks to Noor Alam, Jennifer Fisher, Eric Martin, David Rondel, and David Turnbull for close and exacting reading of my draft manuscript; and to Rob Tempio, my editor at Princeton University Press, who proposed this project, shepherded it through its many stages, and stayed with me. Thanks, Rob; you made me a little less anxious while I wrote this book.

ANXIETY

ANXIETY

OUR AGE(S) OF ANXIETY

Every book on anxiety must, perforce, begin with a list of broad sociological observations and statistics, each showing just how common suffering from anxiety is in contemporary society, and moreover now, how ordinary a fact it is to be medicated, formally or informally, for it. In such fashion are we confronted with the dreadful persistence of anxiety, a seemingly ineradicable aspect of the human condition, for the historical and cultural record of our civilization reveals each human generation has found itself afflicted with forms of extreme anxiety, its peculiar manifestations and expressions characterized by its attendant material culture and circumstances. Sometimes, in reading older descriptions of states of mind evoked by legendary social, cultural, and political crises and comparing them to those reported by our fellow citizens during their tribulations, we notice archaic anxieties have found distinctive, contemporary expression in this era. Many ages have proclaimed themselves a "zenith" of "cultural anxiety," or an "unprecedented" age of anxiety, whether the thirties, the forties, the fifties, the sixties, the noughties; each age imagines—in a distinctive form of rueful self-anointment—that its material, social, and political circumstances have elevated our simmering unease with the very fact of existence into an all-consuming terror. Every age of man, it seems, is an "age of anxiety"; every age plays host to its idiosyncratic monsters of "dread" and "angst" that cloak dimly understood primeval anxieties in their novel garb.

While fear and worry appear grounded in specific objects and circumstances, anxiety is inchoate, a formless dread, a "fear of nothing." Why do we feel it, and must we suffer it? In response, different ages have characterized anxiety differently: as a spiritual crisis of faith, belief, and meaning; a cognitive-behavioral construct resulting from conditioned responses to man's physical and social environments; an animal instinct limited to creatures with a temporal sense who anticipate their own deaths; a response to material stress or society's sexual repressions; a medical affliction of faulty neurophysiology, a problem exclusively of our biology and physical architecture. The Freudian psychoanalytic understanding, equipped with its theoretical notions of the unconscious and a tripartite mind, treats anxiety by resolving inner psychic conflict; contemporary psychiatry and neural science isolate and modify anxiety's biological mechanisms, while philosophical and contemplative traditions seek the *meaning* rather than the *mechanism* of anxiety for its sufferers.[1] Anxiety's sufferers possess an awareness of *finite time* as past, present, and future, and the fear of *unspecifiable future pain or suffering*; anxiety is part biological dysfunction, though the causal link between biology and anxiety remains unclear and unspecified; it is partly a function of our natural and built environments, of the primacy of nurture versus nature; it may indicate an acute spiritual crisis for the believer, a failure to come to terms with faith and the demands of existence; it may be an indicator of a riven and disunified mind haunted by its past; it may be the symptom of an oppressive, alienating culture and society; it may be the very nature of human consciousness.

Anxiety appears to be a universal, perennial human condition, one that remains, despite the impressive onward march of well-funded empirical psychology, pharmacology, and neurophysiology, an equally impressively mysterious phenomenon, one not easily accommodated in, and by, scientific paradigms and frameworks. We do not quite know how and where to slot anxiety in; to pretend otherwise is to be like Sigmund Freud's "wayfarer," who "whistles in the dark" but does not see any the better for doing so.[2] Anxiety's very diversity, its seemingly disparate causes, its manifold complexities and manifestations, reminds us human beings are complex creatures, not mere biological automatons, not creatures exclusively of nature or nurture or class relations or race or gender identities. Anxiety is a frightening reminder we are complex beings not easily resolved into the atoms of our favorite theories.

Our age is perhaps especially anxious because it must confront the technical and material optimism and accomplishment of our times with the sinking feeling that none of it matters very much. The prosperous and powerful are still struck down in midflight, amid their fame and fortune; they can afford expensive doctors, and their lifespans are longer and more comfortable than those of the plebes; they can flee from climate change in their private planes as they outrun a hurricane or a flood; but they, and their loved ones too, succumb just like the rest of us, to cruel misfortune, to biological time bombs of genetic dysfunction, and to terrifying eventuality; they too, receive news of, and bear witness to, the suffering and death of all those they hold near and dear. Upward mobility, "societal success," may enable some to buy their children the best clothes, the best Ivy League education, to arrange for expensive pianoforte lessons, but it cannot protect their most precious possessions against a drunk driver, a plane crash, a fatal disease like a pediatric cancer, creeping climate change, or worst of all, a neuroticism and rejection of this world that manifests itself in acute mental illness, psychopathology, or the self-extinction of suicide. The persistent, nagging realization that our technical and material mastery of nature, our economic power, and our scientific prowess leave our fundamental existential predicaments of mortality and limitation as before is good cause for growing terror; there is "no exit."

Our contemporary perplexities are greater, for we have been fed a diet of progressive and optimistic claims about the unstoppable onward march of science through mental and physical realms and the relentless technological progress toward imagined utopias of plenty; and yet, we still feel an instant regression to profound anxiety at the slightest intimation of mortality: perhaps because, as a well-underway climate change catastrophe suggests, we have realized that these dreams of material advancement, of the mastery of nature, are our nightmares too, driving all we hold dear—like clean skies, drinking water, our children's futures—to the brink of disaster; or perhaps because those modern electronic communication tools, our indispensable playthings, which were supposed to increase mutual knowledge, political empowerment, and empathy, have instead generated political and intellectual dysfunction, and propped up the powerful all over again. Perhaps it is because we sense that no matter how great our mastery of techniques that enable us to polish and buff our material exteriors, we remain in our psychic interiors the same old fearful, uncertain, and anxious creatures.

This ubiquity, this persistence, this presence, provides a clue to the nature of anxiety, its place in our lives, and what we may do about it.

Anxiety bears an acute relationship to philosophy, the oldest of human preoccupations; we are driven to ruminate, to introspect, to philosophize, because we are curious about what afflicts and torments us even when no apparent threat is visible, about why, despite our greatest material successes and comforts and lofty intellectual endeavors, despite achieving all we were expected to, we remain anxious and fearful. Considering philosophy to be a *resource* for anxiety is unsurprising because the philosopher, the lover of wisdom, the archetypal wise person, has long been considered a doctor of the spirit and soul—a "psychotherapist," a healer of the psyche, in the precise etymological sense—an ancient analogy dating to the dawn of the philosophical tradition.[3] Philosophical treatments of afflictions of the soul require metaphysical and moral self-examination, self-discovery, and self-acceptance: philosophy directed at oneself.

But anxiety is not merely a problem for which philosophy offers a solution, an affliction for which philosophy offers a cure. Rather, anxiety and philosophy are intimately related; anxiety is the very "loam" from which philosophy springs and blossoms,[4] for a distinctive form of anxiety, as evinced in philosophical inquiry, is a fundamental human response to our finitude, mortality, and epistemic limitation. Inquiry—the asking of questions, the seeking to dispel uncertainty—responds to this anxiety. The inquiring, questioning, philosophical being is, in a crucial dimension, the anxious being. Anxious creatures philosophize for they are dissatisfied, not content with what they know and believe about the world; they seek to inquire, to remove doubt. What is the nature of our being? What kind of world is this? Is it one in which good is rewarded? Will happiness be realizable in this world? Is this world all there is? What is the nature of the otherworld, the afterlife? What do we not know? Can we ever be certain? Are there truths we will never know? Ethical inquiry reveals an acute *moral anxiety*: Am I doing the right thing? What is the right way to treat others? To live? What if I do not get this right? Our "love of wisdom," our "philo-sophia," is great, but it is not mere idle curiosity that drives it; the answers we seek are remedies for a sense of wonderment and awe tinged with terror. Deep unanswered questions in philosophy, ones to which we sense our answers have immense importance, carry with them great anxiety about the possibility of the "incorrect" answer. Even if anxiety, or "angst," or "dread," or "anguish," is formally named only in the nineteenth century, we can recognize its affect earlier in philosophical writings: a philosopher may describe a species of suffering—spiritual, moral, epistemic—recognizable as anxiety; it lurks between the lines of many expressions of perplexity and awe and uncertainty in the philosophical corpus. And as philosophy paid attention to *those who philosophized* and not just the *doctrines* they produced—what did the inquirer *feel* as she raised these acute epistemic, metaphysical, and moral questions?—anxiety became a philosophical problem in its own right, soon to be understood as an indelible feature of human existence, a constitutive component of human consciousness.

In this work, drawing on the claims of the ancient and modern philosophical traditions of Buddhism, existentialism and existential theology, psychoanalytic theory, and critical theory, I aim to provide a *philosophical guide* to anxiety. As my list of sources indicates, if we do not accept a traditional—and academically and professionally self-serving—trifurcation between psychology, philosophy, and religion, then the range of philosophical speculation about anxiety is increased, for many religious or spiritual injunctions and prescriptions to seek relief from anxiety are philosophical ones in both form and content, and many psychological cures for anxiety are also, in both their foundations and their modality of treatment, philosophical ones.

The debate over *what anxiety is* is not insignificant in the currency of our culture: if deemed a biological and medical phenomenon, a problem of rewiring brains and altering chemical imbalances, the neurophysiological and psychiatric professions stand to gain in intellectual, cultural, and financial capital; if found to be a psychological and behavioral notion, then psychotherapists, clinical psychologists, and sundry counselors and therapists do.[5] My intention here is to point to those philosophical understandings of anxiety that concentrate on the human suffering of anxiety and seek its *meaning*, and do not seek to *reduce* it away by suggesting our anxiety is "nothing but *X*." To tell a patient of anxiety that their suffering is but a physical dysfunction is to do nothing to understand the meaning and significance such dysfunction could have for the sufferer.

What does it mean to provide a philosophical guide to anxiety? First, this is an introduction to *philosophical theories of anxiety*, to what (admittedly, some selected male) philosophers have said about anxiety, hopefully translating their seemingly esoteric concerns into everyday ones, and indicating how to live with it by understanding the role anxiety has in the human condition. The philosophical reflections that the Buddha, Friedrich

Nietzsche, Søren Kierkegaard, Paul Tillich, Martin Heidegger, and Sigmund Freud offer us suggest that to be anxious is to be human and that to be human is to be anxious. Here, anxiety is not always a pathology to be eradicated but often an ineluctable and indispensable part of ourselves; to be anxious is to receive confirmation of our humanity and personhood, an understanding of our place in the world. We are anxious because we are a particular kind of entity, placed into a very particular relationship with the rest of the cosmos. Understanding the nature of our being, and of this relationship, is key to understanding the nature of our anxieties; and vice versa, for understanding our anxieties is to aid our understanding of our being.

In my writing, I will move along a fourfold front. First, I will consider Buddhism as a species of ancient philosophy, self-consciously understood as medicine or therapy, that suggests human anxiety is founded on a deep misunderstanding about ourselves and our natures; our anxiety, which is a species of existential suffering, is undesirable and can and should be eradicated, even though the path to get to that desired end point is long and arduous and requires us to live with and confront anxiety along the way. Second, I will examine the works of some representatives of the nineteenth- and twentieth-century European existentialist tradition who suggest anxiety is the hallmark of freedom and authentic existence and is a privileged gateway to self-discovery and knowledge; we must find a way to live with our anxiety, and indeed, welcome our struggles with it, for the alternative is an inauthentic life lived in "bad faith" where we play at living this life rather than seizing it. Third, I will consider Freudian psychoanalytic theory, which suggests, too, that anxiety is an integral and unavoidable part of the (civilized) human condition, but which locates it proximal to, and as a signal of, external and internal repression and psychological conflict; the repression and the conflict must be acknowledged and integrated into our sense of who we are. Last, I introduce the notions of "materialist alienation" found in the writings of Herbert Marcuse and Karl Marx, who suggest anxiety is a human response to the dehumanizing and alienating material conditions of social life; rather than accepting it, we should strive to (sometimes radically) change the social, political, and cultural world to reduce its anxiety-creating role in our lives. Anxiety arises from who and what we are, how we choose to organize our societies, how we treat others and expect to be treated in turn; a philosophical understanding of anxiety, then, is an existential, political, and moral philosophy.

Bringing these four perspectives named above to bear on anxiety allows us to make the case that anxiety can and should be "cured," but only in a particular way, while we remain appropriately evaluative and skeptical of the man-made forces that conspire to keep us anxious. The bare facts of mortal, limited existence make us anxious and always will, but we do not have to exacerbate our suffering by our reactions to it, or by the social arrangements we construct for ourselves. With this philosophical attitude, we can acknowledge that anxiety is a problem and yet find a measure of acceptance of and resistance to it.

In providing a guide to philosophical theories of anxiety, I will also—implicitly—be describing how to use philosophical *method* of some sort to resolve our suffering of anxiety. Among these resources is a reconceptualization, a recasting of anxiety, via a new philosophical understanding: we re-cognize our fearful, mysterious anxiety, make it comprehensible, understand it differently, through the acquisition of a novel philosophical vision; philosophy can help reclassify anxiety as not a mere pathology but as an essential component of human consciousness, one to be reinterpreted and integrated into our lives. To philosophize about anxiety is to *think* about it, to *reflect* on it, as opposed to merely *reacting* to it, or *suffering* its symptoms; to philosophize about anxiety is to make it possible that we can change the nature of the beast that lives within us because we understand its presence and its role in our lives differently. The result of frank inquiry into our anxiety (and anxieties) can be a heightened awareness of our life and its particular and peculiar challenges, blessings, heartbreaks, and unredeemed promise, bringing about an acute reckoning with the possibly flawed choices, decisions, and actions that have brought us to life's passes; the resultant introspective suffering promises us greater self-understanding and self-acceptance.

The terrible anxiety disorders and panic attacks that many suffer appear impervious though, to philosophical reflection; they seem impervious to reasoned argument and to claims that suggest our anxiety is an essential or unavoidable component of ourselves. To those who suffer so, the suggestion that anxiety might be not pernicious would be offensive; and indeed, the kind of philosophical reflection promulgated here needs, at the least, a mind not afflicted by pathologies that render otherwise clear thought incoherent. For those who suffer in this fashion, anxiety feels like an outsider, a presence that must be banished before their minds can address life's other pressing demands. And yet, even "effective" antianxiety medication cannot ameliorate the fundamental *existential* anxiety (and its variants) described in the pages to follow.

Merely reading sympathetic exegeses of philosophical doctrines, of course, will not result in you putting this book down and saying, "I get it; I do not feel anxious anymore"; a potentially therapeutic philosophical doctrine must make sense emotionally and intellectually too. That happens when there is a measure of congruence between the way you have lived your life and understood and interpreted it, and the way you understand the philosophical claim directed at it. And so, what might happen instead if you think through the claims made in this book and revisit them, even during moments of anxiety, "working through" them, is that you might *understand* and thus *experience* your anxiety differently. And to understand our anxiety, we must experience it not as we are trying to push it away, but as we are trying to inspect it, to see what it "points to." This means that analogizing philosophy to medication can take us only so far, for whatever philosophy is supposed to do for anxiety, it is not there to cure it. But it can offer *understanding*, and thus a *displacement* and possibly a *dissolution* of the problem: what appears to be a problem is no longer one because in the process of reinterpreting it, we have changed its identity and nature. If we come to understand our anxieties differently, we may find we can live with them; we may come to understand ourselves and our preoccupations a little differently, an important contribution to "the examined life," one worth living.

When we examine the histories of the world's greatest psychotherapeutic traditions—psychoanalysis and existential psychotherapy being prominent examples—we find them grounded in philosophical reflection about the human condition; their endeavors are armed with a set of philosophical presumptions and axioms about the human mind and its pathologies. No pioneer in these fields is philosophically unsophisticated in their writings and reflections (the prime example being Freud, of course), and neither are they apologetic about the philosophical foundations they rely on in their therapeutic theorizing. For evidence of the importance of philosophy to modern psychotherapeutic modalities, consider "cognitive behavioral therapy," which claims that the ways in which we think, feel, and behave are not intrinsic to us, but are instead the result of an ongoing, continuing, learning and conditioning process.[6] Within this understanding of psychological dysfunction, persistently "faulty" patterns of thinking and belief formation and revision lead to untenable conclusions and patterns of behavior, which might make us and those who love us unhappy, depressed, and anxious. In response, a species of "intellectual virtue theory," as it were, aims to make us reason better, to help us entertain the "appropriate" emotions guided by the "correct" beliefs, those that "work for us" given our "life goals." Cognitive behavioral therapy is an example of a *philosophical method*— overtly inspired by the ancient philosophical traditions of Stoicism, Buddhism, and Taoism[7]—pressed into service for the treatment of psychological disorders. Its track record in treating anxiety and depression is impressive; the best clinical empirical outcomes in these domains of psychotherapy are often reported from cognitive behavioral therapy.[8] That a species of "cognitive therapy"—which treats the interpretation of our beliefs and the disruption of pernicious patterns of thinking as key therapeutic maneuvers—is an important and often effective treatment in the realm of clinical psychology, and the foundation of a species of philosophical counseling,[9] should establish a prima facie case that philosophy and philosophical reflection have a role to play in ameliorating anxiety—as philosophical writings on anxiety so keenly show.

Philosophically understood, anxiety is a *constitutive* aspect of the human condition, an inevitable response of human consciousness to existence; while the causes of and triggering events for kinds of anxieties vary, we will always find occasion to be anxious. Indeed, if we did not, we might well suspect ourselves of being "abnormal"—for to feel anxious is the "normal" state of humanity. *We will always be anxious, but we do not have to be anxious about being anxious.* This claim, I will argue, mostly by pointing to other philosophers' writings, is empowering rather than debilitating. Anxiety, like so-called addictive behaviors, is not intrinsically a pathology or a disorder. When it is, it is because it has interfered with the kind of life we want to live; but even if we are living the life we want to live, we will find we are not anxiety-free and that reflecting on our anxiety may help us uncover clues to the life we want to continue living.

Those who study anxiety across various disciplines often complain the term is used to describe wildly disparate phenomena: feelings, behaviors, moods, and brain states themselves (the clinical psychologist wants no confusion between her named disorder and the existential mood!)[10] The infamous *Diagnostic and Statistical Manual of Mental Disorders* (*DSM*), the handbook of practicing (and prescribing) psychiatrists, has many afflictions lumped under the category of "anxiety disorders" including "posttraumatic stress disorder," "panic attacks," "obsessive-compulsive disorder," each defined by a hopefully characteristic cluster of symptoms and medicated accordingly. As you read on, consider what you take your anxiety to be and how it manifests itself and how and when the philosophical analyses described here resonates with your own personal experience of it; linguistic and definitional precision is neither necessary nor desirable; what truly matters is your felt experience and understanding of anxiety. Existential, psychoanalytic, or materialist anxiety may seem unlike the affliction named "generalized anxiety disorder," but thinking through the disorder's symptoms and experiences when attached to individual lives may show that the named disorder is the way in which your distinctive version of "philosophical anxiety" finds expression in your life and being.

Those who philosophize often call on philosophy—unapologetically—as a form of therapy, as an aid to navigate life's uncertain contours and trajectories. Reading what philosophers have to say about anxiety will not remove anxiety from our lives, but we may come to understand why we are so anxious, so often, and how anxiety helps us know ourselves. By philosophical reflection on the nature of anxiety, we may obtain an understanding of anxiety and our intimate relationship with it and thus, a measure of acceptance of ourselves. We cannot stop being anxious, but philosophy can help us not be anxious about anxiety.

"A tear is an intellectual thing";[11] so too is a fear, a joy, a regret, an anxiety. But intellects and their complexities are not disembodied entities separable from humans; they are wedded to very particular lives. In this work, I describe, too, my personal relationship to anxiety by way of the study of philosophy and personal philosophical reflection on the role anxiety has played in my life. I will make note of my encounters with anxiety via the perspectives of my history of familial bereavement, my psychotherapeutic sessions, and the relief I experienced on encountering philosophical thought. The most important discovery in this psychotherapeutic and philosophical self-examination was that I had not become anxious because of the trauma of personal loss; rather, I had always been anxious and always would be. I could not therefore be cured, but I could recognize and accept the man in the mirror; my anxiety made me who I am, and I could not get rid of my anxieties without ceasing to be myself.

My personal experiences, my self-indulgent invocation of memoir in the pages to follow, are hopefully of use then in seeing how one person has lived life in response to philosophical claims about anxiety and worked them into their conception of themselves; my life's particulars will differ from yours in significant ways, but hopefully, because we are both human, we will find enough commonality to enable an empathetic bond between us. The bridge we build between philosophical doctrine and our lives depends on the particulars of the individual life, so the way you approach these doctrines depends on your distinctive species of anxiety and your personal interpretational narrative of your life.

In what follows, I hope to point to a path of greater understanding of anxiety and of yourself in turn. This book is an invitation to reflect, to reconsider and reconceptualize anxiety. I promise no cures, because I cannot; I can only offer the thoughts of others like you and me, fellow human beings, in the hope we may find we are not alone in our anxieties. Our suffering is a mark of our humanity, a sign of our membership in the community of humans.

BECOMING AND BEING ANXIOUS

One morning when I was twelve years old, my father died at home. I awoke to a call for help (my name shouted once, loudly, desperately, fearfully, by my mother), ran into my parents' bedroom, and found my father convulsing in the throes of a massive heart attack. His body bucked on a deadly trampoline, his chest heaved, spittle flecked his lips and the sides of his mouth as he desperately sought to fill his lungs with air. By the time our friendly family doctor arrived, stethoscope and black bag in tow, my father was dead. An impossibly handsome Ray Bans–wearing, crew-cut pilot and war hero, he had flown supersonic fighter jets in two wars, evaded antiaircraft fire and airborne interceptors, only to come home and die, not so peacefully, in bed, as his wife and two sons looked on helplessly. Bullets and shells had missed their mark; a clogged artery, a fragment of plaque, had not. He was forty-three years old; I was twelve.

Fourteen years later, after a protracted struggle with breast cancer that included a disfiguring mastectomy, adjuvant chemotherapy, aggressive blasts of directed radiation, hormonal treatment, and a cruel, tantalizing, four-year remission, my mother finally succumbed and passed away into death, into oblivion and nothingness, into the greatest unknown of all. Her last days were painful, mind-numbingly so; she was nauseated, incoherent, delirious, sleepless, her skin yellowed by her failing liver, her lungs crushed by the pathologies that lurked within her. The morphine we asked her doctors to administer to reduce her pain made her catatonic and slowed her pulse to a barely discernible crawl. I had become unrecognizable to her; she to me. She was fifty-two years old; I was twenty-six.

I remember, quite clearly, the day my mother had showed me her cancer, her harbinger of death. There it was, a curious, nondescript region within the CT scan, a zone of irregularity visibly distinct from the cells surrounding it, its shape and shading setting it apart. And yet, it looked of a piece too with its environment, fitting in and making room to exist side by side with the life forces that sustained my mother; thus did I learn that death coexisted with life. My mother's cancer was remote and distant, but most of all it was impervious and indifferent: it just did not care for my grief and sorrow, the horror I felt at impending catastrophe; it did not care for my mother's pains, psychic and physical. It merely worked toward its cellular and molecular teleology, doing what it had to do to flourish, to play its discordant part in its enclosing biological chorus. In its world, my mother and her children did not intrude. We were irrelevant to the cancer's calculi for survival, expansion, and reproduction. It could not care about us; it did not know we existed. If only I could have reached into its membranes and given it a good shake, or written it a strongly worded letter or a longform essay detailing the excellent reasons why my mother should have been allowed to survive—she had suffered too much; she had witnessed her life partner die shockingly and suddenly; she had spent too little time with her year-old grandchild; her younger son was away from home, leaving her alone in the big city for the last six years of her life. Maybe it would have listened, persuaded by my epistolary eloquence and visible pain, my frantic need for my mother to survive, my terror at the thought of a life thrown off course by the trauma of bereavement; perhaps it would have taken pity on two young men who had lost their heroic father just as adolescence crept up on them.

But the cancer would not adopt any of these stances because it could not. Its world was utterly removed from my fears, hopes, desires, and loves. That indifference was terrifying; if the universe had been hostile or malevolent, I could have cursed, fought, strategized; I could have placated it with offerings to satiate its appetite for human lives. But such strivings were beside the point, for the universe was not the sort of thing that responded to human imprecations. We were present in the cosmos, but our home could not be bothered to provide safety or security for us. The universe, if not actively malignant, was indifferent to our fates and cared little for our lives and loves. It did not know, and could not care, that we existed. It could only spit us out and take us back in, in an endless cycle of creation, transformation, and destruction.

When my parents died, a fundamental, metaphysical, sundering between the world and me took place; lightning had struck twice. The gravity the world had promised—the anchoring of my childish flights of anxious fancy—had disappeared; the world was now treacherous, lurking with pitfalls, crevasses, and trapdoors. The world of misfortune was once dimly glimpsed, its details barely visible. I lived in it now; it was mine to occupy. I had imagined that with my father's death, the world had exacted its pound of flesh, reached out, and put the touch on a twelve-year-old, a tax so terrible it would be levied only once. But in fourteen years, death came calling again. That deadly misfortune would be greedy and grasping, unsatiated by the lives it had already claimed, was inconceivable; this world was treacherous beyond comprehension. One God—a child's

God, mythical, compassionate, responsive to prayers—died with my father; another—an adult's God, a God of reasonableness, the one that ensured this world would not do badly by you—died with my mother. I had not killed God, but God had certainly committed a very public suicide by these paired proclamations of His death.

My parents' deaths, occupying polar positions on a spectrum of suddenness, infected my life with a persistent dread; they suffused my life with an incurable anxiety. These grim lessons taught me this world is ruled by merciless probabilities; there are no warnings attached to daybreak that this is the day of catastrophic misfortune, of fatal happenstance. Joan Didion once wrote that recollections of disaster always begin with the mundane nature of the day;[1] the day my father died, the day my mother's cancer was diagnosed, began as ordinary ones before becoming extraordinary and world historical. I learned, the hard way, that there is cause and occasion to fret, to feel anxious, even when there is no indication of disaster; this is a world not made for us, to cater to our desires. From the time I immersed my mother's ashes in the flowing waters of an Indian holy river, I became especially aware of what seemed like a new aspect of my life; new terrors had come into view, more terrifying possibilities were on the horizon. If lightning could strike twice, what was to prevent it from striking repeatedly, finding newer forms of expression, perhaps a distinctive new malignancy with which to infect and corrupt my being? My parents' deaths had opened the portals of fatal possibility; I had glimpsed the terrors that lay beyond.

My anxiety was insidious, more than a simple fear; it was, all at once, a fever and an occupation, an affliction, and a constitution; a lens with which to view the world, a coloration that granted my experiences their distinctive hue. The Buddha alerted us to a fundamental metaphysical feature of this world, the "codependent arising" of all that we experience and know[2]—nothing possesses existence independent of all else that makes it so; an anxious person inhabits a world colored and contoured by their own, highly individual anxieties; it is a world co-constructed by the sufferer and their anxiety. Anxiety is thus a perspective, an interpretive medium allowing a peculiar hermeneutical relationship with the world, whose text now gets read in a very particular way by this anxiety-laden vision. Things and persons and events fall into focus depending on their interactions with our anxieties: that man in the corner becomes threatening; this chair becomes unstable and unbalanced; that food becomes the agent of a future fatal illness; that gesture mocks us; my family—my wife, my daughter—appear tempting targets for cruel twists of fate. I lived in a distinctive world, one shaded and illuminated by the anxiety that was my constant companion and interpreter of existence.

I began psychotherapy at the age of twenty-nine.[3] I had resisted it for the years immediately following my mother's death even as well-meaning friends, hearing me talk about my visibly persistent melancholia, repeatedly recommended that I "see someone." But therapy seemed like a cop-out. My male friends spoke disparagingly of the "culture of whining" it created, the endless childish blaming of parents for adult pathologies. Therapy seemed wimpy, not manly enough, a solution for those not strong enough to deal with life's adversities, who wallowed in self-indulgent pity parties on therapists' couches. I held back, hoping I would "deal with it." But I noticed little change; I easily descended into gloom and doom; I struggled with sleeping too little, with drinking too much, with smoking too much pot, with romantic relationships that foundered on the shoals of rage and jealousy; anxiety and panic were my constant companions. In the fall of 1996, with my doctoral qualifier exams in philosophy creating ample opportunity for questioning my self-worth, I went looking for help.

At the Institute for Contemporary Psychotherapy in Manhattan, after intake interviews, I began therapy twice a week with my assigned therapist. Then too, I considered taking antidepressant medication and consulted a psychiatrist for an evaluation. The good doctor, comfortably ensconced in his plush clinic in Greenwich Village, helpfully informed me he could, if I wanted, prescribe one of the most popular antidepressant medications at the time—Prozac. But panicked and anxious about its legendary side effects and the concomitant banality-inducing sexual dysfunction, I declined medication and continued with my talk therapy. During the five years of interpersonal, psychodynamic, and Kleinian psychotherapy that followed, I realized I had always been an anxious person, that I had not started being anxious after my parents' deaths, that my anxiety marked me out as a fellow sufferer to other anxious humans (i.e., everyone else).

My first therapist was a young woman who listened impassively as I spoke; made anxious by her silences I would continue speaking, quickly and voluminously, till time ran out. I asked for a replacement, someone who would actively interact with me; I wanted confirmation I was not mentally unsound, that I was making sense. In retrospect, I wanted, too, a comforting mother, not a stern father who would ask me to grow up and behave; I was looking for the therapeutic equivalent of a comforting hug, a gentle "there, there, it's going to be alright." My new therapist worked with me for two years, before I broke off therapy after going in circles, a familiar and significant feeling in my encounters with psychotherapy. I found myself returning repeatedly to choices I felt incapable of making, to responsibilities I felt unwilling to take on, to acknowledgments of what was unalterable in myself and the world I inhabited, without being able to reconstrue it. Because I was so often hungover or stoned, my therapy sessions were often a haze; my second therapist's most significant intervention was that she got me to sober up enough to finish my doctoral thesis. Getting rid of my medication of choice meant I felt my anxiety and depression more acutely. I had more to talk about in my therapy sessions as a result.

During therapy, I constructed an archaeology and genealogy of my life, one in which I had often been described as a "sissy" or a "wimp" or a "pussy"—in more than one language—thanks to my overt expressions of anxiety; I remembered my night terrors, my delayed bed-wetting, my feverish panics at the thought of missing a train or a school bus, my shyness ("social anxiety"), my fear of school examinations (whether written or oral), my fears of dogs and heights and deep water and crawling bugs and the dark. If there was a phobia out there, I had it; I feared drowning, falling, being bitten, being late. I had always been fearful, and I had been further terrified; many phobias had lurked within me, forms of deeper anxieties, waiting to be evoked and sustained by this world. It was all too easy to imagine the worst; every road's terminus was catastrophe—that's how this world's workings resolved themselves. I had confronted possibilities and realized that within them lurked fearful actualities that sprang out and revealed themselves; even when they returned to the shadows, their traces lingered. Sometimes, my fearful anxieties had manifested themselves as anger as I raged and raged, appalling my romantic partners, family, and friends; this red mist quickly bottomed out into dark wells of unresolved and undefined terrors.

As I spoke and spoke, my therapists quietly taking notes, offering the occasional comment, or asking for clarifications, I returned time and again to the same perplexing crossroads in my life: unable to move forward, to commit to a course of action, whether it was breaking up with a girlfriend or undertaking a rigorous program of self-improvement; I was apparently anxious about losing an older self and the ambiguous comforts it promised. I talked of jealousy and anxiety, about my fears of loneliness, of abandonment, of losing a girlfriend, of not finding a secure job; I wondered what these losses would signify, what deeper meaning they held for me. I found myself going in circles of repetition, wondering why I could not, would not, move on from points of decision, from points of commitment; these moments of "existential blockage" were sometimes crystallized in failures to end toxic relationships or compromised life situations. I feared being alone, of moving on by myself, of facing the world without a pseudomother (my girlfriends) or a pseudofather (my career, my work, my calling), because I lacked the "existential courage" to move on, to face life by myself, to make decisions that would plunge me into uncertain modes of being.

In seeking therapy, I had thought I would be classified, and treated as, a patient for trauma, but there in the clinic, I found out I was just another person who had always been indecisive, distracted, insecure, or anxious, which, I was quickly learning, *amounted to the same thing*. My anxieties had become worse; my parents' deaths had traumatized a subject primed to be so. Their deaths had interrupted a continuum of development in which I would have separated myself from my parents "naturally"; their premature deaths were "unnatural" with respect to my developmental stages of self-discovery-and-construction; those deaths had threatened values that I held essential to my meaningful and purposeful existence in this world.[4] My parents' deaths made me realize that anxiety is both febrile and fertile, capable of bringing forth newer versions, ever more novel imprints of itself. Prompted by the production of new traumas and losses, the appearances of new threats, my anxieties interacted and recombined—like viruses—to form newer strains that coursed through me, surprising me with their ferocity and visceral feel. My fears had changed, but my primeval anxiety, the dark, forbidding fount of those fears, was the same even as the particulars of my life changed; its bubbles kept rising and taking new form in the worlds I inhabited.

And the worlds I lived in changed in material and affective terms; I became an immigrant, a graduate student, a lover, a professor, a husband, and most dramatically, a father of a young woman. Each role—growing up, getting a job, getting "settled down"—found anxieties and insecurities in new forms. I had gone into therapy seeking relief from depression, grief, distraction, and sexual jealousy—miraculously, they were all related, visible manifestations of a foundational, basement-dwelling anxiety. I was distracted—suffering from a "deficit of attention"—when I read or wrote because those acts made me anxious that I was too stupid, too slow to do so, and was therefore wasting my precious, quickly running-out time on this earth; I was anxious about the books I was not reading (or writing), the life I was living, which seemed impoverished and misguided compared to the ones others were living; I was painfully, pitifully, pathologically jealous of my romantic partners and envious of their sexual histories, because I was anxious about sexual and romantic incompetence, and the resultant failures and losses they signaled; I was depressed because I was anxiously anticipating other losses like the terrible ones I had already incurred, anxious about the possibility my parents' deaths signaled my unerring selection for a variety of misfortunes, signaling to the cosmos I was ripe for the picking. These mental phenomena were varied manifestations of a gnawing, sickening, nauseating dread, made up of a host of inchoate images. I could not bear any more mourning, whether literal or figurative; there was a witness within me, and it had seen enough.

Freud famously suggested the purpose of therapy was to get us from hysterical misery to common unhappiness.[5] Therapy, accordingly, did not assure or comfort or cure me. I had hoped to learn simple trauma had caused my anxiety; I had suffered a blow or a wound, and it would be healed; I could be cured of disease. I learned instead that anxiety was constitutive of my being; I could not be described, even to myself, without describing my anxiety. My psychic location as a young Indian man afflicted by postcolonial angst and resentment; my childhood as the younger son of a larger-than-life father, an aviator and warrior who had survived two wars and seemed invincible; my beautiful, loving mother's widowing, her subsequent traumatized depression and fatal illness; my fraught relationship with my older, bigger, and stronger brother (a fighter pilot, no less!), whose attempts to become a surrogate father I deeply resented and resisted; my insecure relationships with my more experienced girlfriends; my migration to a foreign land whose hypermasculinity was destined to intersect unfavorably with my less obvious masculinity, whose hyperindividuality and socially atomized state could not welcome a lonely, homesick exile seeking home; my decision to seek out a profession—academia—marked by intense emotional and psychic insecurity, spiritual isolation, and relentless competition: these particulars contributed to, flavored, and signed off on my distinctive, highly particularized dose of anxiety.

These empirical details of my life intersected with the bare particulars of the fact that I am a mortal human being, one possessed of imperfect knowledge, of incomplete and unrealized abilities. I am not omniscient, therefore I am anxious because I do not know what may come my way; I am not omnipotent, therefore I am anxious because I know I cannot and will not withstand all the insults, physical and mental, the world sends my way; I am not omnibenevolent, so I am made anxious, for I know and sense that I am capable of wrongdoing, of malevolence, of doing harm even to those I love and care for. I am reminded by my incapacities, too, that I might be victim to other humans' failures of benevolence and knowledge. The more I gain in this world, the more I make myself anxious, because I have more to lose. When I was young, I was possessed by deep anxiety over the life yet to be lived, whether I *would* live it "correctly"; now that I am a middle-aged man, I am racked by anxiety over whether I *have* lived my life in the correct fashion. I found joy in my life through the existence of my precocious, beautiful daughter, yet this silver cloud is lined with black, my happiness over her presence in my life tempered by the terrifying possibility of her loss while I am still alive. In middle age, my anxieties about death and decrepitude, about the pain and discomfort that lies ahead, about inflicting my disrepair and death on my family, have taken on a darker hue.

Life seems a cruel trick designed to generate and sustain anxiety.

Death taught me much about anxiety and who we were. Death's early presence had ensured that every loss in my life—migration across the proverbial black water included—would be colored by the deadly fear evoked by the most terrible losses of all, those of my parents; nothing has been quite as formative of my emotional and philosophical dispositions as those twinned blows. The slightest intimation of loss, no matter how utterly mundane, was an invitation to be traumatized all over again. My fear of death made death and death anxiety vividly present in my life. I created, facilitated, and participated in mini-deaths: I drank till I blacked out, drinking, and sometimes driving, as fast as possible, to achieve oblivion; when I lost my temper, I raged so spectacularly I could feel the red mist turning black, sending me into a pleasurable haze, an oblivion that delivered me momentarily from anxiety. My rage was the simple converse of a desire to sink down in a heap, bawling, curled up in a corner, terrified of the misfortunes this world could send my way. I became convinced, and remain so, that I will die in one of the two ways that brought down my parents: I will collapse suddenly, brought down by a cardiac arrest, or I will notice a lump in my body, get tested, and find out I am dying of cancer. Both possibilities terrify me equally; the latter perhaps more so because it promises more pain and suffering, especially that engendered by the reactions of my loved ones, who will stand by my deathbed, stroke my feverish brow, hold my hand, and weep as I slip away into the land of no return.

My parents' deaths had made me feel cursed, touched by the malignant and contagious hand of fate; I realized, too, that they had brought me into contact with unacknowledged aspects of our gross, bodily existence. My father's facial expressions as he had fought for breath; his inert body covered by a white sheet stained by the traces of excreta expelled by his sphincter muscles loosening at the moment of death; the flesh on my father's body crumbling and melting as it disappeared into the flames of the funeral pyre; my mother's yellowing skin as her failing liver pumped toxins into her blood; her crushed lungs, her nausea and vertigo, her drifting into oblivion over her last few days. I had left my mother's body in the hospital morgue overnight, leaving her alone in that house of the dead, trying to convince myself that that body was not her, unable to fully move past the horror that had gripped my disbelieving heart. Had she been conscious of being alone, of missing her two sons, trapped in that dark, morbid, cold repository? I had noticed that as death approached, my mother had vanished, to be replaced by an inert body; I learned about the dissolution of self and personality as her body broke down, a deep, fundamental philosophical lesson I imbibed without textual analysis. I could see, inexorably, stage after stage appear in her, each caused by the one before it; then, a life I recognized was over, a person I knew was gone. But the physical traces of that presence remained, to haunt me with their resemblance to the one who brought me into this world.

After my mother passed away, a fundamental crisis overcame me; I realized that I was free as never before. Till then, I had understood my life as bound up with my parents; perhaps I had to aspire to their standards, seek their approval, live life less recklessly because of their sensitivities; now, all such barriers were removed; I was free, as the song goes, to "do what I want, any old time."[6] I could put myself out of my misery, end my existence, secure in the knowledge my parents would not have to grieve the loss of their precious son. This realization provoked appalling terror; it was the first time I experienced dread, as I understood what philosophical existentialists alluded to in their descriptions of our "dreadful freedom" and its resultant anxiety. If there was a God, it had been my parents, and their deaths had taken my moral order, my purpose, my raison d'être with it. What was I living for? Whom was I living for? What was the point of all of this if I had no one to share it with? If my parents could die in such brutal, uncaring fashion, so could my brother, nephew, wife, daughter, friends, and me. What then of all I had and stood to lose?

The upending of this world's order by my parents' deaths and my anxious state of being made me suffer a conceptual shift in my understanding of its workings; it became a philosophical commonplace for me to believe claims about this world's malleability through our conscious, emotional, not entirely rational understanding of it—because that was my experience, for the world and I had changed in tandem once my parents died. Because I lived in a world of uncertainty, certainty in any domain seemed laughable; I would look at the arrogant strut of my uncaring fellow humans and think one blow would bring them to their knees. The fragility of the human and not-human, man-made or not, was starkly visible; living life was reckless effrontery. My parents' deaths taught me that this world was quicksand built on quicksand; that talk of certainty was laughable; that all things came to be and passed away; that this world contained many worlds within it, which continued to exist even as others terminated; that God did not exist; that there were no truths more vital than love; that all we wanted was companionship and spiritual solace. I found myself drawn to philosophical theories that assured me there was no meaning or value to life save the ones we gave it, ones that told me there was no predetermined purpose to my existence. To believe that there was a predetermined end to my life, a destination, an intended teleology, was to be infected with an anxiety that I was not fulfilling my purpose in life, that I was wasting my life. That anxiety could be relieved only by convincing myself this life was purposeless, that I could not snatch defeat from the jaws of victory. Curiously enough, this thought was more sustaining than airy directives for how to seek out the Truth about Reality and Being. It put the wind beneath my wings; that this world had no particular purpose, no end in mind for my life, was an intoxicating and relieving possibility. I could just live.

I had found psychotherapy around the time I sought to become a professional philosopher; my philosophical education therefore had a role to play in my working through anxiety; it, as much as my sessions on the couch, was my therapy. I discovered formal philosophy in two forms: there was philosophy that seemed technical and abstruse, and that which seemed personal and emotional. The former was the classical canon of "modern philosophers" and "analytical philosophers"; they squabbled, aggressively and pointedly, about theories of meaning and the nature of existence and mind and language and knowledge, about theories of reference, and consciousness, and semantics, and the conceptual foundations of physics and biology; they imagined themselves critical commentators on the physical and social sciences, and that was it. Philosophy was a critical, inquiring observer of the world, an activity performed not by human beings but by schools of thought. The identity of the philosopher was irrelevant; what mattered were the doctrines she produced. So impersonal were those doctrines that I felt absent; they were irrelevant to my life, to the reasons I had chosen to study philosophy. I wanted philosophy to help me with grief, with anxiety, with understanding why my life was the way it was.

Among the latter group of philosophers were the existentialists: Jean-Paul Sartre, Friedrich Nietzsche, Søren Kierkegaard, Albert Camus, Miguel Unamuno, Fyodor Dostoyevsky, among others—some of these worthies were not considered philosophers by the academic world and did not feature on its reading lists. In this company, I found allowance for, and acceptance of, my suffering, my acute desire for this cruel and meaningless world to make sense. The existentialists were melancholic and introspective, concerned to understand why they felt the way they did; they wrote openly and honestly about death and the absurdity it threatened our lives with. I was aware that I—like other human beings—was a curious hybrid of emotion and intellect; existentialism, a hybrid of philosophy and literature, of emotion and intellect too, reassured me that within abstract philosophical speculation lurked real human beings, concrete creatures of flesh and blood, not abstract instantiations of favored theories, and certainly not just technical analyses of arcane philosophical minutiae. The existentialists spoke of moods, and feelings and emotions; they made claims about the human condition that were autobiographical, that bridged the gaps between literature and philosophy and psychology and even religion and spirituality. Their claims were a matter of them reading their moods and those of others; they did not arrive at them through intricate, pedantic chains of arguments. Only an existentialist like Kierkegaard could have said, "Science too, as much as poetry and art, assumes a mood on the parts of both producer and recipient."[7] They made me see new things and old things anew; they made me feel different when I started reading philosophy. They made it clear that comprehension and realization of philosophical claims followed on the heels of our ability to emotionally accept them, and that moreover, if you did *truly* comprehend something, you could come to feel the appropriate emotion too; as Kierkegaard insisted, some subjects (and their importance in our lives) could be understood only if you entertained the appropriate moods and emotions.[8] Their formulations connected philosophical thought to the business of how we ought to live: to fully and properly understand something we thought was a matter of trying to live according to what we thought. I had come to the right place; here I would find what I needed to live, not to "succeed," "do well," or be "upwardly mobile," but to live—even if not always happily or free of anxiety.

My first reaction then, on encountering existentialist formulations of existence preceding essence, of the absurdity and meaninglessness of existence, was relief. I did not feel terror at the possibility life was meaningless or absurd; I had already received empirical confirmation of that claim. My parents were dead, a signal that there was no limit to this world's cruelty; their deaths had rendered absurd this world, exposed its deliverances as a cruel lie, a fatal misrepresentation. But *neither was I cursed, picked out for punishment by the cosmos*; my parents' deaths were not evidence of a preemptive strike; they were, instead, events that could have happened to anyone, and whose importance and meaning within my life was a matter of the interpretation I placed on them; after all, if the universe truly were as nonsensical as it seemed to be, why would it be so particularly interested in my fortunes? My anxieties about future misfortunes had been condensed into the fear my life was on the wrong track, a fear sustained by familial, social, and cultural expectations and transmuted into a cosmic constraint: you must live your life in this fashion, in this manner. Even if I was not bound for heaven or hell, secular punishment and scorn—forged without the wisdom of God's beneficence—awaited me: I had wasted my potential, made the wrong choice of career, settled for the wrong life partner, and was living the wrong life in the wrong way. The greatest failure of all awaited me, that of having lived my life incorrectly. Life was formless, but even more terrifying was the possibility of colossal normative failure. Existentialism promised relief from that ghastly possibility; there could be no wrong decisions. I had to find my part, my own, decided by me. There was not a role written out for me to play in my life, one I was failing to live up to; there was not a normative blueprint for living I had failed to instantiate. I, whatever I was, was a matter of invention, not discovery.

The first deliverance that philosophy had promised me was simple occupation of my time: I felt more alive, more simulated, less anxious, while I was reading philosophy (well, at least the well-written variants). It was possible that the glow would go away once I put the text down, but some of it persisted, coloring my subsequent interpretations of life's events, and enabling me to understand them through a new philosophical vision. Second, philosophy did give me a detached view *species sub aeternatis*—an elevated "view from nowhere" that rendered insignificant petty worries and fears pertaining to the weekday by placing them into more expansive relief. And finally, philosophical doctrines like existentialism provided psychic comfort; by showing me how life's humdrum decisions were infected by the "ultimate concerns"[9] they intersected with, they showed me there was nothing mundane about these decisions and preoccupations; each one was bringing me into contact with a primeval anxiety and deserved respect accordingly.

By raising—but not remaining content with—the possibility of this life's meaninglessness, existentialist doctrines had eased the terrible, anxiety-provoking thought of a preexistent meaning and value and essence not discoverable or realizable by me. In a world with no wrong decisions, there would not be the anxieties of cognitive dissonance, of wrongly lived lives either. I realized the therapeutic value of such philosophizing and embraced it. My anxious state made me receptive to it; it prepared the intellectual ground by saturating it with an emotional and affective field built and sustained by an acute anxiety. Philosophy done in this therapeutic fashion is not a shameful state of affairs; it is precisely as it should be: philosophy employed to teach us a better way to live, to dispel those illusions and delusions that make this life harder than it needs to be.

I came to philosophy seeking relief from melancholy and anxiety and the processing of my grief. I did not think I would find a solution in philosophy; I merely hoped I would have time to read, to lose myself in the printed word and the hard-earned wisdom of others, a virtuous whiling away of the time, the best way to run down the clock on a life that seemed unlivable and unbearable in the enervating offices and company that came with a nine-to-five schedule. After years of study, as a student, a philosophy professor, and now a philosophical counselor, I find my anxiety has not gone away. I must live with it—it is a vital component of my ever-evolving self. In finding acceptance of myself, I especially consider how my anxiety could be a distinctive expression of myself, how it has made me live the life I currently do, and thus determines who I am. I hope philosophy can be of similar service to you, that it can help you accept that we will always feel anxiety, that we do not have to be anxious about being anxious.

Philosophy is not an abstract doctrine, a career, a means of winning arguments, a way of sounding worldly, esoteric, or sophisticated, but a living prescription that speaks from and to the heart and the mind. Philosophy has made a difference in my life; I rely on reading and thinking through philosophy, and on nonpharmaceutical prescriptions like meditation, hiking, climbing, running, and weightlifting, to help me "work through" my anxiety. Not "conquer," not "heal," not "cure"; I hold no hope that such will be my relationship to my anxiety. The words I use instead are "accepting," "living with," and, if you wanted to get more colloquial, "owning." My anxiety is not alien or external; it is mine; it is me. My guide for bringing me to this realization was philosophy and my life informing each other. I hope this book will do the same for you.

THE ANXIETIES OF EXISTENCE

The ancient religion and practices of Buddhism show philosophy as a practical, moral, and therapeutic enterprise, offering "vehicles for self-transformation" and "practical solutions" to its adherents' "keenly felt experience of suffering";[1] the explicit task for a philosophical therapy based on Buddhism is to offer "treatment of deep-seated dissatisfaction."[2] This is an ambitious task, and the complexities of Buddhist doctrines (there are several), and their rigorous demands, are geared to ensuring that self-transformation and personalized practical solutions find keen expression in Buddhist theory and praxis alike.[3] The notion of "treatment" invoked here reminds us the Buddha was understood by his disciples as a doctor, "the Great Physician" who offered diagnoses, prognoses, and prescriptions to "cure the spiritual ills of the suffering world."[4]

Foremost among the "spiritual ills" that cause human beings "deep-seated dissatisfaction" is the complex and frequently misunderstood Buddhist concept of *dukkha*. While dukkha is sometimes understood as mere "suffering," an examination of its nature and its putative causes reveals it to be—besides other affects and feelings—an acute anxiety, an existential discomfort, resulting from an intellectual and emotional failure to face up to the bare facts of existence (which include the nature of human personal identity). We can read the Buddha as claiming that to be alive—and crucially, deluded—is to be anxious, grieving, fearful, and angry; our first step toward relief is a true, unblinking understanding of the nature of the world and of human existence's place in it. If we misunderstand the nature of the world and more importantly, ourselves—mistake that rope for a snake or vice versa—we will be anxious, and suffer, in ways far worse than we need to.

The Buddha taught an acute understanding and acceptance of the world and of our personal identity; once you understood how it "worked" and who and what you were, then human dukkha stood revealed as a species of unnecessary suffering, grounded in a deep, fundamental, metaphysical misunderstanding of the nature of reality. Misplace yourself in this conception of the world, and you would suffer; correct this vision, and you could rescue yourself from a species of acute existential suffering. Buddhism, then, considers anxiety—like anger—a disease to be cured; its practices aim to ameliorate and minimize its impact in our lives. The Buddha claimed that "tranquility" of a very particular kind could be attained by "changing the beliefs on which emotional turbulence depends"[5] and offered to his followers, beyond the construction and evaluation of philosophical arguments (an enduring hallmark of the animated discussions between the Buddha and his disciples), a variety of techniques to achieve such states of mind that include "efforts to calm the mind, close observation of mental states, modification of habits, anticipation, postponement, distraction, advice or consolation, invocation of role-models, self-examination and confession."[6] These instructions and methods survive into the modern day; every popular self-help book on anxiety includes some variant or the other of these fundamental spiritual exercises. The tranquility these practices offer though—if taken to their intended end states—is "the complete or near complete absence of emotions such as anger, fear and grief."[7] We might not desire such an affectless life, given the often desirable political and moral valence of emotions like anger, a complication in the acceptance of Buddhism by those seeking nonmonastic modes of life. But the path to this promised tranquility is one worth traveling if it promises *some* relief from a very particular kind of suffering that afflicts us.

For the Buddha, anxiety was a problem, the emotion engendered in a situation when a being like us is deluded about what it is, and about the nature of the world it inhabits; anxiety is an unfortunate affliction to be avoided and cured by altering the terms of this relationship with existence. As we will soon see, while this attitude toward anxiety distinguishes Buddhism from existentialist treatments, they will significantly agree that what causes anxiety is our acute conscious or sublimated awareness of our death, our mortality, our finite life, our decidedly human constraints and constitutive conditions. The contrast between these two understandings of anxiety is that when we are enlightened by Buddhism and realize our true natures, we will be free of anxiety, whereas when so by existentialism we will embrace our anxiety to understand our true natures. But in both cases, we must not shy away from anxiety: in the case of Buddhism, by understanding what causes it, and how our misunderstandings lie at its roots. This requires that we inspect the nature of the beast (our mind) at close range, via mindfulness or meditation techniques that allow us a first-person study of consciousness to inspect our thoughts and understand their relationship to whatever we take ourselves to be.

To understand the Buddhist notion of anxiety, consider the Four Noble Truths, which the Buddha offered to his disciples as antidotes to this world's perplexities: There is suffering in this world; this suffering has an identifiable cause; this suffering can be eased; here is how you do so. Buddhism's First Noble Truth notes the undeniable, acute human dissatisfaction with existence, an indelible component of which is dukkha. The Buddha then noted that our first step toward relief, as expressed by his Second Noble Truth, that our suffering has a cause, is a true, unblinking understanding of the nature of the world and of human existence's place in it. Our suffering is not mysterious and inexplicable; it is grounded in the bare facts of human existence. To understand it, we must unflinchingly accept the nature of the human condition, its finiteness, limitation, and circumscription by the metaphysical particulars of the world. Buddhism then tenders us the injunction that our emotional reactions to the world must be cognizant of, pay attention to, what we realize and know about its nature; our emotional reaction to suffering, loss, and pain must be tempered by this hard-earned insight and realistic appraisal of the relationship of our suffering to the constraints existence places on us.

The Buddha was never pessimistic about our prospects for deliverance and salvation; a view of Buddhism notable in the West as an unrelieved pessimism, a species of world nausea or world rejection, is profoundly mistaken.[8] The Buddha instead offered an optimistic prognosis via the Third Noble Truth: suffering can be eased via the Eight-Fold Path revealed in the Fourth Noble Truth, a combination of mental attitudes, stances, and importantly, commitments and practices, geared toward the development of habits that let us live life more "skillfully." Buddhism's promise is that we can ease our suffering, our dukkha, our anxiety, by transforming the way we perceive and cognize the world; we can achieve salvation or deliverance, attain the blissful state of *nirvana*, through a form of awakening or "coming to see," a long, slow process of removing those hindrances from our mind that have blocked us from seeing what and who we really are; it was this "failure to see" that underwrites our anxiety. As the Buddha noted, "suffering by unsatisfactoriness of unenlightened existence" can be avoided by "transformative insight" or being able to "see and know things as they truly are." The many therapeutic maneuvers to aid such seeing that the Buddha recommended for his disciples along the Eight-Fold Path of Action and Righteous Duty issue in movements from being an unskilled practitioner of life's arts to being a skilled one, from being one who is perpetually, miserably seasick on a long journey across the oceans to one who learns to walk with ease, across a slippery and tilting deck on a leaky boat crossing a vast, deep, stormy sea. The person who does so is equipped with both a knowledge of the physical particulars of the deck, and an acute knowledge of their own personal capacities; these are then artfully blended in the practice of "skillful balanced walking."

An unthinking, glib reaction to the Four Noble Truths of Buddhism is that they are banal and commonplace. But we still do not show any inclination to take them on board; we claim they are obvious, and yet we do not respond, through thought and deed, to their truth. By way of analogy, consider someone who is blind and has undergone an eye operation to restore sight. When the bandages are taken off, we ask them if they can see. They reply "yes" but then promptly walk into a table in front of them. So, they do not see yet. Or consider someone who goes to see a movie and begins crying and wailing as the titles flash up. When we tell them to collect themselves and leave, for the show is over and the next one about to begin, they refuse to leave; we would say they do not understand what a movie is, how it is supposed to work and end. We would say they need to be familiarized with the concept of a "movie" so that they can relate to it in a way that does not cause them as much discomfort in their encounters with it. Such is our situation with respect to our understanding of the nature of reality, and our place within it. (It will not do in response to this analogy to suggest the movie viewer is simply being "emotional" or "overwrought"; the Buddha would suggest that if such emotions cause us discomfort, then we must marry them with the understanding of *what a movie is* and what watching it entails.)

Dukkha is acute existential suffering. Dukkha is not the mere expression of discomfort at this world's varied empirical misfortunes like the loss of a job or an income, or the physical pain and discomfort of illness and injury; it is not simple fear either of visible, identifiable threats like a snarling animal or a poisonous snake on our path. We know that this is so because even if jobs, incomes, secure housing, pain-and-illness-free days were to be secured, and dangerous animals neutered, we would still feel dukkha, for that feeling is the acute suffering of the sentient being confronted with the impermanence and transience of its lived world, with ignorance about its true self, and with the intractable difficulty of satisfying its endless, easily frustrated desires. The existential suffering we experience is grounded in the "the frustration, alienation and despair that result from the realization of our own mortality."[9] We are frustrated because we cannot finish our life's projects or ever hope to reap their rewards in perpetuity; all such enjoyment must be limited by time tinged with fear of their loss. We cannot, during any given pleasurable state, avoid feeling that the state will end soon, to be replaced by its deprivation, or that we will grow sated, and begin longing, hopelessly and helplessly, for the lost desirable state. (Indeed, such pleasurable states, like beautiful days in the spring or fall, make us especially anxious as we dread their all-too-soon ending, their vulnerability to "wasting" by us, their possibly-never-to-be-repeated status.) We experience alienation because we feel estranged in this world, in both the political and the economic realms, which are controlled and administered by forces not under our control or reckoning, and in the private realm, where we are alone and isolated in our unique, incommunicable, ineffable subjectivity, one that can never be made satisfactorily commensurate with anyone else's. Ironically, this extreme isolation is most evident when we are in love and notice that even those whom we love the most, like our parents, our romantic partners, and our offspring, will remain at a deeply significant level, utter strangers. We are in despair because we realize we are limited and mortal, in life, in capacity, in achievement; we glimpse a Promised Land and know that it is impossible, materially or physically, that we should ever attain it; we sense we are powerless, in the face of nature, to prevent harm being done to those we love, and to ourselves; we cannot halt the inevitable progress of time, disease, decay, and death. (The American pragmatist William James, that most sensitive of philosophers, made note of "a horrible dread at the pit of my stomach, a sense of the insecurity of life"; this ineliminable sense, arising from our painful awareness of the tolls this world exacts, underwrites our dukkha.[10] The inescapability of pain and loss, and our deep instinctive awareness and knowledge of it, no matter how well disguised, brings James's understanding of his psychic afflictions close to the Buddhist formulation of dukkha.)

The day my daughter was born, I rejoiced, even as I acknowledged facts almost too painful for me to make note of here: that I cannot prevent her from suffering loss and despair of her own; that none of the force of my parental love and longing can change the nature of the world she has been born into; and finally, and shatteringly, that she too will pass someday. I hope I will not be alive then even as I realize that in so hoping, I am hoping only one of us will have to bear the pain of the other's passing. These dark thoughts we must play with are the perennial shadows in our lives, ones no human being no matter how rich, powerful, and desirable, can avoid. We strive to leave our mark, to be memorable, but our fate—of especial interest to beings who cannot stop asking what comes next—is oblivion. What then, of this world and all its demands?

For the Buddhist, existential anxiety is a species of dukkha; it is not neurosis; it is not a sign of freedom, authenticity, or the limitless possibility of action and choice. Instead, it is the state of being of an ignorant creature confused about its own nature, fumbling in the dark, hurting itself and others by its delusions and ignorance, by its fearful reactions to the ever-present possibility of decay, dissolution, and death in its life. The anxiety, the dukkha, it suffers from is pointless and needless and can and should be alleviated or eliminated.

For the Buddha, there are three failures of knowledge and realization that underwrite our dukkha. First, that the world is transient and dynamic, ever changing, and never stable, perpetually productive of uncertainty, resulting in our instability, emotional and physical, in the face of its unexpected challenges. (The suggestion that the world is always changing, that the present moment is ephemeral and fleeting, can be a source of comfort too, of course, for "this, too, shall pass.") Second, this perpetual becoming, a naturalistic expression of the world's physical dynamism, ensures that our desires cannot be satisfied permanently because enduring, safe satisfaction can take place only in a world that affords places of repose, rest, and quiescence. I might desire and procure an ice cream cone, but even as I eat it, I am aware both that this pleasurable sensation will end, and moreover, that I will attain, if it does in fact continue, a point of fullness, for all satisfaction of desires is followed by satiation, boredom, or anxiety about loss of the desired possession—of whatever form, whether tangible or otherwise. This "suffering by way of transformation" ensures we are beings caught in a species of acute psychic and emotional insecurity. (These formulations of the unstable satiation of our desires would appear later in the work of the German philosopher Arthur Schopenhauer, who fulsomely acknowledged his debt to Eastern religions and philosophy. Schopenhauer is sometimes termed the "most pessimistic" of philosophers, for he realizes the satisfaction of a wish is merely a prompt that another take its place, that in pursuing our never-ending wants and desires, we are doomed to swing between desperate grasping, satiation, and boredom.)

We suffer, then, because our awareness is tainted and soiled by the knowledge that our happiness depends on an unstable, dynamic, ever-becoming world that does not lie within our control; we are aware, whether consciously or not, that happiness is fleeting, that all possessions, tangible or otherwise, are threatened by loss. Of the many variants of anxiety, this one corrupts and destroys even our rare moments of joy and pleasure, for we are aware that any happiness procured at great emotional and physical labor could end at any given second, for reasons that become understood only once we have experienced them. The unknown, the formless, and the unknowable conspire to render our present contentment hollow, for we realize it will end at some point in the not-so-distant future and, indeed, could easily morph into its exact opposite. We thus live in a state of awareness at various levels of the fragility of existence, of uncertainty over whether our happiness will be taken away, of the fates of our loved ones, and all we hold dear; this knowledge is acutely painful. We know we can sense the black lining of the silver cloud; we are aware decrepitude, loss, death, and deprivation always lurk close by. Our experience of this ineliminable awareness is dukkha. Within this Buddhist understanding, antianxiety medication misses the mark completely, for it cannot cure our suffering from grief or anger, nor can it diminish our awareness of the inevitability of death, or diminish our grasping, our thirst, our desiring for this world's impermanent, transient goods and joys.

For the Buddha, we especially suffer from ignorance about *who we are*, for the selves we imagine ourselves to be do not exist in the way we imagine them to; we remain deluded and suffering so long as we are ignorant of "the thesis of non-self." This last point, the third and final failure of knowledge that ensures our suffering, is the most esoteric and certainly the most contested of Buddhist doctrines; it is, too, the most fundamental and the most important in Buddhist teachings, as the Buddha persistently suggested. To wit, we are anxious because we are worried about the fate of a particular thing or object, our self, the precious "I" (the one to whom our body belongs when we say "my body"). It is this self's losses, its misfortunes, its apprehension of the nothingness that ensues after death that cause our anxiety; it is this self's fortunes, its gains and fame, that we seek and strive for. The Buddha however, offered a deconstructive and deflationary analysis of personal identity to dismiss the notion of a an enduring-and-identical-through-time "I," an ego, or a soul, that functions as a locus for our anxiety, and, in the social and moral worlds we inhabit, as a locus for moral and legal blame, agency, and responsibility.

In the Buddhist view, we are made up instead of five persistently and rapidly changing "bundles" or "heaps" or "piles" of body (form), sensation, perception, volition, and consciousness; but there is no enduring "I" here. The "I," such as it is, is a rapidly morphing stage of persisting dynamic processes and consists of parts that are not "I" themselves. All there is to us is these five dynamic bundles; we are animated bags of blood and flesh and water with a particular form that sense and feel and move and are conscious, but there is no one enduring entity to whom this belongs; none of these things makes up the exalted "I" or "individual." We are sites, the loci of where these five dynamic processes meet and form a visible unity over an extended period; each stage of this process causally produces the next one, but there is no enduring entity. We possess form, sensation, perception, volition, and consciousness; and nowhere in here will an enduring self be found.

But this self is the entity that is the locus of our fears and worries; it is this, to which we give a name through elaborate christening ceremonies, whose welfare we are concerned with, whose body we aim to protect from external insult and injury, whose fortunes and misfortunes cause us happiness and sorrow; it is this self's passing into nothingness we mourn and fear. So deep and grounded is our attachment to the self that till we pay systematic attention to our thoughts we do not notice that while we have thoughts they are not attached to any owner; the content of our thoughts is other thoughts; the presence of such higher-order thoughts, it turns out, is what it means for "thinking" to take place. And if there is no owner of these thoughts, this body, then why are we concerned about fate, loss, fortune, reward, and gain, which acquire meaning and significance only when attached to someone or something that gains or loses by them? Our suffering is the way it is because we are confused about who we are, and who others are. So long as the center of our concerns remains the "I," or "ego," or the "self," we will remain ensnared in this world's bindings, which can offer only temptation and unsated desire, and the inevitable pain, disease, suffering, and death of the mortal. The conventional "I" is distinct, separated from the cosmos, a fundamental sundering that places us apart from the rest of "all there is"; the Buddhist vision of the nonexistent self returns us to its swirling midst, there to take our rightful place with the rest of creation. We are not distinct and separate, cast out to be ourselves; we are always one with the One. We are not strangers cast out into the world; we never left and will not go anywhere when we die. (This vision of cosmic unity or "oneness" is reported by those on psychedelic journeys; for those in hospice care, such experiences can be deeply comforting, as they promise death can be a return and transformation, not an extinguishment and effacement.)

This notion of the supposedly eternal, immortal, and immaterial self being a linguistic convenience, a handle of sorts that we attach to a rapidly changing entity (much as we insist on using an enduring name like "Liverpool Football Club" to refer to a sports team with perennially changing personnel), is on display in this famous, oft-quoted, and oft-cited dialogue from the Buddhist canon, between the Indian king Milinda and a traveling Buddhist monk, Nàgasena:

MILINDA: How is your reverence known, and what sir, is your name?

NÀGASENA: O king, I am known as Nàgasena but that is only a designation in common use, for no permanent individual can be found.

MILINDA: If, most venerable Nàgasena, that is true ... then there is neither merit nor demerit, nor is there any doer of good or evil deeds and no result of karma. You say that you are called Nàgasena; now what is that Nàgasena? Is it the hair? Is it then the nails, teeth, skin or other parts of the body? Or is it the body, or feelings, or perceptions, or formations, or consciousness? Is it these combined? Or is it something outside of them that is Nàgasena?

NÀGASENA: It is none of these.

MILINDA: Then, I can discover no Nàgasena. Nàgasena is an empty sound. Who is it we see before us? It is a falsehood that your reverence has spoken.

NÀGASENA: You, sir. How did you come here, by foot or in a chariot?

MILINDA: In a chariot, venerable sir.

NÀGASENA: Then, explain sir, what that is. Is it the axle? Or the wheels, or the chassis, or reins, or yoke that is the chariot? Is it these combined, or is it something apart from them?

MILINDA: It is none of these things, venerable sir.

NÀGASENA: Then, sir, this chariot is an empty sound. You spoke falsely when you said that you came here in a chariot.

MILINDA: Venerable sir, I have spoken the truth. It is because it has all these parts that it comes under the term chariot.

NÀGASENA: Sir, it is because of the five aggregates of being that I come under the term "Nàgasena." Just as it is by the existence of the various parts that the word "Chariot" is used, just so is it that when the aggregates of being are there we talk of a being.[11]

For the Buddha, the anxious person was ignorant and deluded, clinging on to, grasping at, a quicksilver, ever-morphing reality, holding on for dear life to transient, ever-becoming possessions belonging to a nonexistent being. The anxiety we suffer in the Buddhist view is entirely explicable: we are always fearful of loss, of the possibility of all the insults the world can send our way, by the transience of all that we possess and hold dear. Looking ahead, we can foresee our own painful disease, decrepitude, and decay—each associated with a particular self, the "I," the ego, me, given a particular name by my parents. Our resultant existential thirst, arising out of ignorance of our state of no-self, grasps at, desires, forms desperate, doomed attachments to "sense-pleasures, wealth, and power ... ideas and ideals, views, opinions, theories, conceptions and beliefs."[12] (Notice that the Buddha does not distinguish between grasping at tangible or intangible goods; attachment to ideologies, to rigid ways of thinking and acting and being, will hurt as much as attachment to material goods and wealth.) This means a relentless growth of "desire, the will to be, to exist, to re-exist, to become more and more, to grow more and more, to accumulate more and more."[13] But such accumulations and possessions are precisely what is threatened by this eternally becoming, uncertain world we have no control over; so, we are always anxious.

Anxiety, then, arises within us; it is not caused by the world outside. The world is what it is; our relationship to it, our knowledge of it, causes our anxiety. Our minds are its creators; when we attempt to remove the object—some empirical threat—that causes fear and anxiety, we fail in attempting to control something other than our mind. If the world cannot be changed, if its dynamism and uncertainty is beyond our control, and if we cannot numb our senses, then all we can do is master our cognitive responses to the world: how we react to, interpret, and judge the world's offerings or insults.[14]

To do so, the first step is to pay attention to how the mind works, to study how the mind reacts to objects of fear, to irritations, insults, interruptions, deprivations, and losses. This heightened awareness of the interactions of mind and body is to be gained by disciplined, regular practices of directed meditation and mindfulness, a first-person study of our consciousness achieved by withdrawing our attention from this world's distractions to ourselves; this awareness makes us concentrate on the present moment, thus enabling us to distance ourselves from regretting or remorsefully remembering the past, or fearfully and anxiously anticipating the future. The Buddha thus asked us to pay attention to our minds, the venues and sites of happiness, sorrow, anxiety, or pleasure; our true, exalted subject of study is ourselves; we should find out who and what we are to understand why we feel and think the way we do. Mindfulness and meditation—achieved via a variety of nontrivial techniques and practices that require steadfast commitment and discipline—enable us to study our thoughts; once we understand our relationship to our thoughts, we may understand we are not hostage to them; we may come to realize that these are "thoughts without a thinker." (Such practices remove, too, our panicky, selfish, self-centered attention from ourselves, from our daily worries; ironically, for something popularly understood as a calming exercise, meditation is a profound *disruption* of our normal ways and means of anxious self-centered thinking.)

Placing the solution for living with anxiety in our minds is simultaneously disheartening and promising: relief is so close, yet the proximity a mirage because the road to deliverance is long and tedious, for the Buddhist methods of mindfulness and meditation require an extraordinary effort for the attainment of the promised state of nirvana, placing them out of reach of most layfolk, a problem acknowledged by the Buddha himself, who offered multiple layers of analysis and practice in his sermons to his disciples, depending on their commitment to the life of enlightenment; not every poor soul who attended the Buddha's sermons intended to become a mendicant or a monk, begging for alms, seeking the life of solitary contemplation. This suggests that while we may never reach the terminus of deliverance and salvation, we must accept, and live with, anxiety. We do not turn back from encounters with anxiety; we face up to it.[15]

Buddhist teachers therefore repeatedly emphasize living with our anxiety; they insist on mastering anxiety, not by avoiding it, but rather by accepting the inevitability of uncertainty, by having faith in our historically oft-tested ability to navigate the expected by-products of a dynamic, always-becoming world.[16] As the Buddhist nun Pema Chodron puts it in many elegant ways:

> We explore the reality and unpredictability of insecurity and pain, and we try not to push it away.[17]

> A warrior accepts that we can never know what will happen to us next.... The truth is that we can never avoid uncertainty. This not-knowing is part of the adventure. It's also what makes us afraid.[18]

> The central question ... is not how we avoid uncertainty and fear but how we relate to discomfort.[19]

> With practice ... we learn to stay with ... with a nameless fear.[20]

> We fear losing our illusion of security—that's what makes us anxious. We fear being confused and not knowing which way to turn.[21]

> Egolessness is ... our capacity to relax with not knowing, not figuring everything out, with not being at all sure about who we are, or who anyone else is, either.[22]

In Buddhism's injunction to acknowledge the presence of suffering as a condition of life, the most straightforward and transparent claim of all, I found great simplicity: there is suffering; so long as we are ignorant, we will continue to suffer. This felt chastising too, for I felt blamed for my suffering; my thinking was the root of my discomfort in this world. But Buddhism's prognosis and diagnosis, its optimism about the possibility of cure, its provision of a path of conduct defined by explicit practices that reached into every corner of the lived life, was also deeply, powerfully empowering: I was the architect of my destiny, the creator of my fate, provided I understood who or what I was.

As a child, I had naively imagined there would be no suffering in this world, lulled into a false security by my parent's comforting upbringing and nurturing, their apparent mastery of the cosmos. I had been disappointed, in the worst way of all, by the disappearance of those guardians, by the acute visible evidence that they were not permanent and indestructible. The failure of humanity, like mine, was a neurotic failure to face up to the constitutive features of existence; its stubborn refusal to accept existence's stern demands was the reason for its misery. In Buddhism, I found an injunction to move on from a childish understanding of the world, to see it shorn of wistful illusion, of narcissistic self-serving delusion. Buddhism's more esoteric claims—ones that the Scottish philosopher David Hume would rediscover in his masterwork of modern philosophy *A Treatise of Human Nature*—that there was no self, just a bundle of perceptions and sensations to be found via introspection, did not resonate with my felt experiences, though its truth became apparent during my psychedelic experimentations, where I found—like the author Michael Pollan did during his ayahuasca ceremonies—that my self dissolved into the world around me.[23] (This was what modern physics promised me too; I was star dust and I would return to that form once this mode of being in the world was done and, er, dusted.) This sheer nothingness of the self was what puzzled the Buddha's devotees, who asked repeatedly and persistently, "What happens to me after death?" In response, the Buddha insisted that this question was malformed; it simply did not fit the case; it was a category mistake. For a nonexistent self, the question of its survival or extinction or misfortunes did not arise.[24]

Even if we never fully attain this state of belief in the thesis of no-self, our contemplative practices that force our attention on the content of the Four Noble Truths may enable us to at least maintain an ironic—and possibly even amused—distance from the very idea of an enduring, identical self that can permanently possess any of this endlessly becoming world's always-changing-and-destructible goods. Perhaps this is why the reclining or seated Buddha is always depicted with a faint smile on his face. He knows "what's up" and "what time it is"; he can look on this world's play and the delusions of its inhabitants with a gaze of amused detachment, one yet filled with compassion for his fellow sufferers.

For the Buddha, anxiety and suffering arise from dispositions, tendencies, and habits; our salvation lies in retraining ourselves through slow, resolute, patient, and persistent effort over the course of a lifetime; our engagement in this activity is our reward and deliverance. We are never trying to seek an end point, a stage at which we will be miraculously delivered from anxiety. It is the act of working on ourselves that is our only deliverance; we are never to be brought anywhere, to any resting point of final repose. Our journey will be suffused with anxiety; we must accept this companion while we walk on, into life.

FREE TO BE ANXIOUS

Our existence is the philosophical problem par excellence: we do not know our way about, and we have not been supplied with a map.[1] And if we ever were thus supplied, by religion, God, and revelation, we have since been informed by science, by philosophy, by intellectual and conceptual revolutions that those maps were made only by human beings like us—confused, disoriented, anxious—and not by an omniscient supernatural authority. The existentialists welcome, affirm, and celebrate our resultant uncertainty, our discombobulation, and its concomitant anxiety, the agonizing, inescapable spur to self-and-world-inquiry.[2] The existentialists sought not to cure or eliminate anxiety; they sought to live with it, even welcome it as a sign of the authentically lived life, one truly in contact with existence's unrelenting demands. In the formulations of the existentialists, we find both the horrors of primeval anxiety—as the manifold translations of "anxiety" as "dread," "angst," "anguish," "foreboding," and "agony" in the existentialist corpus suggest—and its liberatory aspects, the opportunities it provides for self-discovery, an authentic life, and an acceptance of an acute moral and metaphysical responsibility for our actions and commitments.

For the existentialists, anxiety was the bridge between philosophy and psychology. Existentialism thus, crucially, forced attention on the moods and feelings that accompanied human decisions and inferences. Those who philosophize are human; we reason and feel and emote; these feelings underwrite the portentous philosophies we generate, turning them into confessionals and autobiographies and self-reckonings. Our emotions and reason are thus inseparable, our gross empirical, profane body and our transient, shifting, indeterminate moods as important as dispassionate, abstract reason; we are alienated and cast adrift when our thinking and feeling selves are divorced. The existentialists therefore made little distinction between psychological investigation and philosophical speculation and inquiry and allowed anxiety, an emotion, to be considered a philosophical issue; their writings crystallized intuitions about the human condition long held and entertained by philosophers, theologians, writers, and poets and provided them new literary and philosophical form; they introduced an acute psychological sophistication and frankness to philosophical analysis that is the hallmark of nineteenth- and twentieth-century philosophy in the Western tradition.[3]

For the existentialists, a cluster of concepts, the so-called ultimate concerns,[4] went together: freedom, death, nothingness, responsibility, authenticity. To think about one was to find paths to others, each paved by anxiety about its terminus, its ongoing progression: our metaphysical freedom to choose underwrote our anxiety over the possibility of moral or empirical error, our taking on responsibility for our actions, our search for authentic existence; the ever presence of death in our lives was a reminder of the cessation of possibility, of the unknowable nothingness that lay beyond, marking an insuperable barrier to worldly aspiration and hope. Despite their diversity of writing styles, theoretical formulations, and concerns, the existentialists were united by their insistence that "man"—whatever or whoever that was—was made, decided, invented, and constructed, not discovered, or found with a predetermined essence and life plan. In our primal states before creation and birth, we await definition, identification, and classification; there is no preexisting essence awaiting realization. The persistent, enduring state of such a provisional being—always worked on, never complete, never quiescent, always becoming, "a stranger in a strange land" aware of death as a looming certainty, of unrealized possibility and eventual nothingness as a constant presence during life—was anxiety.

The existentialists were acutely aware of and sensitive to a foundational fact about the human condition: we—even the wisest and most knowledgeable and powerful—are *uncertain* of what the future will bring. The existentialists considered this pregnant uncertainty evidence of a world and self yet unmade, of the *freedom* of choice and action that we "enjoy." Freedom is our prize, our medal, our anointment for the state we find ourselves in, the perplexity that confronts us. Freedom is a prized moral and political good; it is, too, a valorized existential good for the relief it promises from a future already written out with roles and essences defined. In our unreflective moments, we crave this freedom, considering a predetermined life that of an automaton. But this freedom comes with the price of anxiety-inducing uncertainty.

The existentialists thus named anxiety as an indispensable part of our understanding of ourselves as free beings, devoid of some predetermined and established essence, and left responsible for our self-creation; to be free is to experience anxiety because we must reckon with making choices that determine the contours of our lives and our fates; the uncertainty of a freely acting and choosing being and its associated anxiety becomes constitutive of human existence and consciousness. Our freedom though, does not feel like a blessing or deliverance; instead, it feels like terror, dread, angst. Much of our lives are consumed by the burdens of anxiously avoiding or denying this freedom; small wonder that we flee into the arms of someone or something, social, intellectual, or even pharmacological, that can reduce our freedom so that we may feel less of its accursed blessing; we are endlessly inventive in fleeing from the freedom of deciding how we should and could live our lives.[5]

For many educated laypersons, the pipe-smoking, coffee-drinking, French philosopher Jean-Paul Sartre is the premier existentialist. For good reason: he offered pithy formulas to express existentialist ideas and expressed its central theses with brilliance and precision through philosophical treatises (including the notably difficult and obscure *Being and Nothingness*) and novels and plays. Sartre is often considered theoretically dependent on his predecessor philosophers Søren Kierkegaard and Martin Heidegger for his notions of human freedom, consciousness, existential absurdity, and nothingness. But more readers have learned about these concepts from Sartre than from Heidegger or Kierkegaard; and his writings on inauthenticity and "bad faith" are especially more quoted. (Some of this popularity is due to Sartre's usage of literary forms to express his claims; his novel *Nausea* and his play *No Exit* are cultural icons of a particular time, their most memorable lines easily deployable on future occasions.) Sartre is sometimes popularly regarded as the fountainhead of existentialism because his formula (or slogan) "existence precedes essence" crystallized a central existential insight: we are not born to instantiate a predetermined metaphysical essence, a perfect, abstract, Platonic Form of which I am only an imperfect realization; rather, I exist, come into being first, and then make myself. My life is the record of my attempts to construct myself by my decisions and choices; I find out who I am as I go along, making myself up. The end of history is the moment of revelation when I find out what my acts and choices have made my life and myself into; indeed, this is when mankind finds out what the nature of "man" is. This unrolling is not a discovery of a preexistent script; instead, we witness man coming to be, through his own making, in time.

Sartre's existentialism is a humanist atheism, for man and his consciousness, and not a Divine Entity, are the determinants of this world. Man begins as "nothingness," not a coin whose value has been stamped on his being for once and forever, and makes not just himself but all humanity through his actions and choices.[6] The world we step into is made by other humans like us; when we leave it, we will have added our pebble to the pile, visible for all to see; these in turn will prepare the world for the next consciousness like ours. There is no transcendental, external authority—like God or an abstract, impersonal cosmic order—regulating, determining, and evaluating this world; man is the measure of all things, and there are no eternal truths—moral or spiritual—independent of man making them so. This places an awesome responsibility on us for the collective totality of humanity, as we understand it, is the sum of individual actions and choices; with every action and choice I place a brick in the wall of this edifice, serving as an exemplar every time I make a choice and take an action.[7] Sartre suggested such inescapable, unavoidable freedom was a "condemnation" to invent ourselves and man.[8] This is an *existential responsibility* thrust on us, far weightier than the gene-based species reproduction demanded by our biology, which can be done unthinkingly as a mere physical impulse. We find ourselves "thrown" into a particular place and time, not of our choosing, but in which we must act and choose to make it distinctively ours. We awaken to find ourselves in this world; our place in it, the meaning of it all, will be determined by us; we are *compelled* to do so.[9]

Freedom's possession, because it is characterized by anxiety, is not an unmitigated joy; we flee by acting, skillfully and convincingly, to satisfy others' established expectations and normative standards. In this "normal" state, I am the self the world wants me to be; I imagine this to be my freedom because I have bought, uncritically, the peddled, socially dominant version. This grants me a stable self, a recognizable identity, a refuge in a zone of made-up comfort; it gives me an acting script I can crib from for my daily performances in this world. But this acceptance of conformity is an act of "bad faith," of inauthenticity, for by seeking safe, sheltered, and circumscribed situations, we find not freedom, but constriction and restraint. These social arrangements have assuaged someone else's anxiety, forcing us into preexisting containers of action and thought, there to wallow in our distinctive misery and anxiety as we find ourselves "outsiders" and "strangers" in a world we have not made or chosen.

For the existentialists, by paying attention to anxiety and acknowledging it not as pathology, we welcome it as a message that informs us of the possibilities of our lives, of the uncertain and not yet decided future to be determined by us, of our most prized possessions and our most terrible burdens. There would be little to no anxiety if our lives were mapped out with trajectories and actions articulated for us to follow, with fates and fortunes predetermined and predestined; on life's stages, our lines would be visible on giant teleprompters; and we would fearlessly speak without fear of retribution and adverse consequence. But, as that old bumper sticker goes, "This is life; this is not a test. If this were a test, you would have been told where to go and what to do." Our anxiety informs us this is terribly true.

The so-called Christian existentialists like Søren Kierkegaard and Paul Tillich chose (a variant of traditional religious) faith as their response to existential anxiety. Common to the existential Christian and the secular and profane solution to anxiety is the making of a choice, a leap of faith, to unswerving commitment, to work, to articles of faith, to people and persons, to a greater beyond, to God, to national or societal tasks. Both resolutions of anxiety require a decision to accept that while all will be mystery, we make headway by taking one mystery as solved. What am I to do next? What should I do? What will happen? We do not know; we cannot be sure. But we can act—with no guarantee of success—and make concrete the previously abstract. This pushing on headlong into the indeterminate, making it determinate with our choices, is our lot and our only path forward. Refusal here is a refusal to live. The more we commit, the more we leave behind the unresolved and disdained parts of ourselves, for to commit, to make a choice, is to cultivate some aspects of our selves and not others. Along with this commitment undergirded by decision and choice is a willingness to live with the consequences of our resolution, trusting that when the moment arises, we will find our path onward.

Ironically for a man who wrote volubly and prolifically on Marxism, Sartre's version of existentialism was dismissed as bourgeois or libertarian for glibly insisting on the primacy and availability of choice to all regardless of socioeconomic class, gender, or race. What of human history, its contingencies, and the acts and choices that preceded ours, building the world in a particular way so that only some choices are visible to, or feasible for, some of us? What of the privileges of choice and possibility it awards to a select well-placed few, leaving the rest of us to anxiously ponder our limited choices? Sartre's philosophical understanding of mankind's freedom appeared then as an excessively, naively optimistic take on human possibility given history and the political and economic arrangements of the world—a critique Sartre acknowledged in his many revisions of his original claims, which noted that our choices, as those of others who preceded us, make the world for those who follow. Yet, there are important insights in his work about the constructive aspects of our decisions and choices and of the centrality of individual responsibility in living our life, in any plans to remake or save ourselves.

As we examine the thoughts of existentialists on anxiety, we find considerable commonality and divergences. Despite the suspicion raised above—and to be revisited—that existentialist thought overexalts the choice and freedom of isolated individuals, treating social creatures as atoms, we find pointed, perceptive acknowledgments of the role that social structures, institutions, and arrangements play in generating and sustaining our distinctive forms of anxiety. The sharpest such critique is by a philosopher considered the theoretical forebear of twentieth-century existentialism and modern critical theory, whose works have long infuriated and exhilarated generations of readers: Friedrich Nietzsche.

The Death of Certainty

Mankind's stark cosmic terror at the bare, undeniable facts of existence had once been offered relief by organized religion, by its doctrines and rituals and required beliefs; it had provided a comprehensive behavioral and moral code regulating every aspect of human life, all backed up by divine sanction. But when such theistic relief was no longer available, thanks to the impertinence of science and the uncomfortable speculations of modern philosophy, what then of the moral and metaphysical guidance of God, religion, and their appointed deputies, the priests and the interpreters of holy revelations? This problem is raised most acutely and famously in Friedrich Nietzsche's writings; the approaching "storms" he repeatedly warns Europe and European culture of are an outbreak of acute anxiety, of depressive nihilism, of repressed, neuroticized, resistance to a Godless world, of desperate eager flight into the arms of "new idols" like the nation-state, the stock market, and sundry ideologies demanding intellectual and moral acquiescence. Anxieties lurk throughout Nietzsche's writings: the anxiety of the religious and nonreligious alike confronted with "God's death" is the most central, for "God" here functions not just as divine creator and moral guarantor, but as the symbol of absolute safe certainty in the moral, epistemic, and spiritual realms, no more to be found in this secularized world of ours.

Nietzsche considered our anxiety to arise from our attempts to be someone other than what we are, selfless bundles of perpetual becoming—a theoretical view that curiously and ironically aligns his theses with central Buddhist claims[10]—our attempts to not accept that this world was devoid of the spiritual comforts that older religious traditions and faith in God provided. It was this failure of self-acceptance, this inability to take on the world with an optimistic pessimism, that was the ground of our anxiety, that turned us into timorous, cowering cowards, beaten down by that which we could neither change nor accept through the construction of a uniquely personal perspective on life that made this world's demands tractable. Nietzsche bade us love our fates, calling out to anyone who would listen that we must accept our identities, our stations in life, our anxieties, as parts of ourselves; by accepting the lessons of the classical Greek tragedies, which, he suggested, expressed a stirring defiance in the face of this world's unsparing requirements, we could acknowledge this world's horrors unflinchingly and find within them the means to confront existence's insuperable challenges.[11] In doing so we could find a means of overcoming ourselves, the greatest task of all.

Most centrally, Nietzsche suggested that our anxiety arises because we are in the thrall of a pernicious make-believe, a self-serving construction and arrangement of the world and its affairs posited and established by someone else taking care of their psychic, moral, and emotional needs as the winner of a "will to power" among all; like the Buddha, Nietzsche considered us to be in the grip of a formidable illusion, one that made us unhappier than we needed to be. To see what Nietzsche is getting at, note that the world we step into has a history of actions and choices made by other humans like us who have modified and constructed it—via an acute, historically located struggle and contestation, sometimes political, sometimes cultural, sometimes psychological, for power—into one that suits them, that satisfies their aspirations, that maintains their stations in life. It is *their constraints, their values, their norms* that we are worried, anxious, and guilty about not satisfying. As a damning consequence, our historically constructed social systems of values, morals, and normative constraints create and sustain an acute anxiety (via a terribly afflicting, guilt-inducing "bad conscience") about not living up to the ideals we imagine regulate our lives. A skeptical critical tradition—going back to Plato's *Republic* and whose modern members include Karl Marx and Michel Foucault—has long suggested that such values and ideals are those whose adoption will ensure the continued maintenance of power of the most privileged and entrenched classes.[12] Morality itself—a specified and regulated code of conduct complete with notions of "guilt" and "wrongdoing," "good" and "evil"—is exposed as an ideology that suits the interest of the powerful. The conscience it instills in us, the unsparing moral self-critique and examination it urges on us? An invitation to guilt and anxiety.

For Nietzsche, power is a diverse concept;[13] but being able to divert and subsume the interests of others to our own is an acute and visible manifestation of it. (So is the ability to subsume ourselves to ourselves!) If the "weak" can make the "strong" do their bidding—for whatever reason—then it is the "weak" who are actually "powerful." This is a lesson every cowed employee, every minion, every person and citizen subject to abstract and multiply realized power learns painfully. (This is a lesson parents often learn from their stubborn children too.) The man wagging his finger at you might be physically unprepossessing, but if he wields legal or financial or state power, he can bring you to your knees, begging for mercy. So can the controllers of culture, the arbiters of moral taste, for they can make you and your children think in the ways they want you to—and can breed a sense of acute guilt and moral failure and anxiety when we do not.

We will, then, not only suffer like the Buddha suggested, for we are mere human beings confronted with our mortality and limitation, but we will also moralize our suffering—a devastatingly self-flagellatory act—by considering this world's socially constructed misfortunes either to be the curse of malignant fates and vengeful deities impervious to our prayers, or to result from our failures of choices and blessings. Our anxiety is our profoundly mistaken sense of living a marginal, failed life, one lived on someone else's terms, all without us knowing that we are doing so; it has arisen from our failure to assert our own will on this world, to make it bend to our needs. This is not a task that Nietzsche imagines all of us as being capable of undertaking; many are the bleating, meek members of the "herd," and few are those independent, defiant, self-reliant "noble souls" who can break free of the herd's demands and imperatives.[14]

If conventional morality is exposed by Nietzsche as a pernicious, anxiety-creating ideology, then so are our social and economic arrangements, the desirable roles that they create, and that we fail to fit into. Here lurk many moral, spiritual, and personal failures of self-realization, all while we remain unaware that these cosmic failures of ours are only so within a particular religious, cultural, or moral perspective, the handiwork of other humans, "all-too-human" just like us. Nietzsche thus suggests that our spiritual illness, our anxiety, *is a function of us failing to find someone else's "life solution" a viable one for us*. But without conventional notions of morality, without their metaphysical and epistemic certainty, with traditional normative values undermined and corroded, we would find ourselves saddled with an awesome responsibility: we must erect new scales for good and bad, new units of measurement, new "tables of values":[15] we and we alone, with no cosmic guidance at hand. The uncertainty we confront is all consuming and immense, tremendously productive of anxiety, for where are we to find normative guidance now? Yet, bear this dread we must if we are to step into the new, fearful, yet promising world of intellectual disillusionment.

"God's death," then, exposes us to existential absurdity and anxiety; if God is no longer available as an absolute guarantor of moral order, of rewards for good deeds and punishment for bad ones, then where is there a corrective to, and balm for, this world's miseries? We are confronted with the terrifying possibility that not only do we lack a grounded definition of good and bad, but we have also lost the protection of supernatural benevolent powers and are left defenseless and powerless against the vicissitudes of fate. There is no promised land waiting us; no final accounting of good and bad deeds; no reward for good acts, and no punishment for sins either. With no judgement sitting on us from on high, we are left without a guide or corrective, a disorienting and terrifying state of being, a constant accompaniment to the ostensibly calm face we present to the world. (A resonance will arise here later with Paul Tillich's notion of the "anxiety of meaninglessness," which is grounded in our fear of "the loss of... a meaning which gives meaning to all meanings."[16] God once was that meaning, which underwrote our existence with reward, reassurance, blame, and praise—if God is dead, "the meaning which gave meaning to all meanings" is dead too.[17])

For Nietzsche, anxiety is a sign of a weak, pessimistic, and unhealthy refusal to accept the world as it is; the brave among us step forward to accept life's challenges, the possibility that this world has meaning only as an "aesthetic phenomenon,"[18] a spectacle of sound and fury that signified only once we made it ours; the "herd" shrinks from doing so. Nietzsche worried about the disaffected and dangerous nihilism that could be a consequence of a loss of faith in God—or metaphysical certainty, for a spiritual and moral abyss yawned ahead. In a meaningless and absurd cosmos, why would we act or express ourselves in any way? Our "highest values" of culture and morality are grounded in axiomatic claims about the nature of the world; what happens when those claims are posited as false? If our highest values are revealed as possessing feet of clay, what would be the point of conformity with them? Why take the slightest action to construct ourselves or our lives if none of this has any meaning or enduring significance, or fails to fit into any larger cosmic scheme? The resultant meaninglessness and vacuity and the self-extinction that beckons bring with it a terrible anxiety; we are aware the power to do so lies within us; it is we who stay our hand. Nietzsche accurately forecast the twentieth century coming of totalitarianism, of excessive reverence for nationalism,[19] of blind slavish obedience to new human or ideological prophets; these medications eased the pain of this desacralized world, making life bearable in it: at the cost of a life sunk in despair, unable to redeem its metaphysical and existential promise; at the cost of a world made worse for those who inhabit it.

Nietzsche exhilarates his readers with his welcomes of the new age, his gleeful acceptance of the challenges that lie ahead, his injunctions that we regard ourselves as artists engaged in the creation of unique and distinctive works of our lives and ourselves;[20] it does not hurt the sometimes-conflicting claims he makes that his muscular and coruscating prose threatens to overrun any pedantic technical objections that might arise. Reading Nietzsche can be an antidote to anxiety just because we are confronted with a mind that resided in a body that suffered terribly (as his many biographies reveal)[21] but who never let himself be intellectually or morally confined by this world's demands. (Modern academics—and corporate workers stuck in "burn-out jobs"—can only envy his utter self-assuredness and confidence in stepping away from the sinecure of a secure university position to set off on a literal and figurative solitary quest across Europe to address the philosophical questions that tormented him.) Those moral and social demands, Nietzsche sensed, were deeply angst producing; they threatened us with damnation and perdition at every step of our lives. They provided security too, a scaffolding of expectations and constraints, which when removed left us uncertain and anxious. The flip side of this teetering state was exhilaration at the exposure below, the sheerness of the fall, the beauty of the novel sights visible from this new vantage position.

Nietzsche's doctrines amount to a distinctive take on our anxiety-causing, fearful mortality—for he suggests it is our friend.[22] The immortality promised by conventional Christian religious doctrine had always come with a price, the possibility of an afterlife of the condemned or redeemed, a tremendous and terrible eventuality that demanded the correct choices be made, the correct life be lived, for "the salvation of poor 'eternal souls' depended [on the] knowledge acquired during a short lifetime. . . . 'Knowledge' took on a dreadful importance."[23] But what if we disdained belief in such immortality and rested content with our moment in the sun? Mortality seems to place a terrible burden on us: anxiety about the unredeemed life, the incomplete, underachieving life, the one that did not find its *summum bonum* during our living years. But finiteness and limitation are our friends too; with the clock running out we may find sympathetic ears when we announce we cannot be bothered taking on too much for this poor, short, all too easily terminated life, this mere blink of an eye. Can any serious projects, existential or intellectual, be undertaken in such a brief repose from the eternal waits of the prenatal and the afterlife? Much as we might curse death and the interruption it induces in our life's plans, Nietzsche suggests, we are secretly grateful; we have been saved by the cosmic bell. No more being looked at impatiently and askance as we clumsily toil away at our pitiful life projects; we must down tools when Death comes calling; indeed, why not down tools right away when we know that the bell could ring any second? We are especially comforted when our mortality is combined with the absence of the Great Examiner who might otherwise have been imagined placed in charge of grading our lives. Our incomplete, unfinished work will not be evaluated or critiqued; it, like us, will pass into blissful anonymity.

Nietzsche rightly makes note above of the relief promised by our mortality, by God's death: there will be no assessment from on high of this ridiculously short life, one in which the "right" or "correct" knowledge could not be obtained within its pitifully short specifications. The "dreadful importance" of this brief preparation for the long immortality of the soul is mercifully negated, relieving us, partially, of our cosmic anxiety. Investing the world and our life with the terrible significance of immortality comes with a burden all its own; the disproportion between the immortality of the soul, that majestic eternity, and the miserable petty shortness of the life meant as testing ground had always seemed radically unfair; deliverance by death into the void is a great relief, an escape, from such existential burdens.

Nietzsche thus cleverly suggests that immortality, without adequate instructions for the journey, may be the greatest curse of all; mortality the greatest blessing. The mortal life returns to its humble specifications—it is no longer a prized microsecond of respite from the darkness, one artfully constructed to give us the opportunity to settle down for immortality. Instead, it is what it has always seemed: a meaningless interruption with no significance in some invisible cosmic schemata, one that awaits investment with meaningfulness by the living of our unique life. Our awareness of our own mortality now leads to responsible acceptance of our existence and its many imperfections, understood as blessings, for our imagination comes to a halt when confronted with the possibility of immortality and how, given infinite time, we could lead a meaningful life. We realize being bounded and finite founds our understanding of ourselves—tasks must be completed, projects undertaken; success and failure become markers associated with work; none of these should matter to an immortal being. We could and should embrace and not dread the inevitable cessation of this life, to fully understand and come to live with ourselves.

For Nietzsche, anxiety was either our reaction to the burden of the world's normative pressures, for creating a sense of guilt and moral failure, or a reaction to their absence, for without them we were lost and disoriented; in either case, anxiety was our resultant state. This absurdity suggested the liberated man was the one who did not need those values, and was not oppressed by their presence or absence, for he made his own, delivering himself to his own demands, and living his own life. Such a state could be free of the anxiety that possessed the common man, but it was, for that reason, an aristocratic state accessible only to a select few, the "noble souls," those who could be "Übermenschen," or "overmen," who could rise above the herd, and make an evolutionary advance toward a higher state of being. Such humans were hardly humans; they were to man what man was to an ape.[24]

Though Nietzsche does not mention anxiety (or "angst") specifically, his doctrines, in conjunction with materialist understandings of anxiety like those of Karl Marx and Herbert Marcuse, provide us powerful critical tools with which to undermine and deflate those man-made-and-sustained structures that are anxiety generating in our political, social, and economic circumstances. For this reason, Nietzsche is a philosopher who can be read profitably by the masses, even if Nietzsche did not have most of us in mind when he wrote his works. He offers us polemics with which we can mount potentially liberatory, radical critiques of the most established of ideologies and political systems, but he is not a democrat; far from it, he is an unrepentant aristocrat committed to a hierarchy of human types, who sneers at the notion of social democracy and of taking care of the weak and the underprivileged.

But Nietzsche's imagined ideals for the good life are aspirational, and we could do worse than try to live our lives like the "noble souls" Nietzsche wrote his works for, for if we did, we would live our lives free of the neurotic fear of disapproval by family, society, and culture, free of the anxiety of losing their love and acceptance, of not gaining their hollow accolades; we would not be racked by guilt just because we were not appropriately deferential to established authority; we would be fully accepting of ourselves, weaknesses and strengths and character blemishes included, as we would take these to constitute our distinctive signature, ours alone, and thereby be delivered from malignant envy and feelings of inferiority; we would disdain devious manipulation of, or sycophancy or servility to, people or ideals; we would realize that while the world lacked meaning, we could construct it and our life in our own unique, distinctive way; we would affirm life to the extent that we would be willing to live this life again and again till infinity as a form of the "eternal recurrence";[25] we would accept our life wholeheartedly, proud and unashamed of all our mistakes, sins, and errors, just as we are of our achievements and medals, for we would realize they all stand and fall together; we would not feel shame or envy or jealousy or guilt or resentment or a desire for retribution and vengeance because these are the hallmarks of the "lower soul."

Nietzsche's deep insight was that the pathological emotions—jealousy, anger, resentment, depression, the vindictive desire for retribution—are underwritten by an acute sense of moral and spiritual and social failure, and the guilt and anxiety that those failures brought in their wake. To reject the orderings and arrangements that placed such failure-causing demands on us was to do no less than to assert ourselves on this world, to shake ourselves free of our life-dominating ideologies, and to set about the formidable task of overcoming and constructing ourselves and our new values.

Nietzsche died alone and insane, his work misunderstood and marginalized and barely read, his own life the most uncompromising exemplar of the ideals he sought to inculcate in his readers. Take from him what you will, what you need. He would be happy to have students and readers in this modern era, to find evidence of his continued relevance in a dynamically changing world, to have made you courageous in the face of your own distinctive anxiety. Especially if it bent you, the reader, to his "will to power."

Faith, Spiritual Deliverance, and *The Concept of Anxiety*

The patron saint of Danish angst Søren Kierkegaard, the intellectual forebear of generations of psychologists and psychotherapists, of the foundations of psychoanalysis (as acknowledged by Sigmund Freud's successors, if not Freud himself), and of his fellow existentialists, including Paul Tillich, Martin Heidegger, and Jean-Paul Sartre,[26] suggested that mankind's greatest "blessing," our freedom of willing and choosing, came with a terrible burden: encounters with anxiety.[27] This burden, Kierkegaard claimed, was one we should happily bear; it is our cross, and we will find ourselves by our willingness to go forth with it, along the paths of our choosing, as we live with the unease of the unrealized universe of our lives. In moments of quiet self-reflection and intense attention paid to the terrible possibilities of our choices, our confrontations with anxiety hold the possibilities of innovative self-discovery: what are we capable of; what may we do; will we have the strength to bear up to the consequences, intended or otherwise, of our actions? To move on with our lives, constructing ourselves despite the discomfort of these encounters, is, for Kierkegaard, the basis of selfhood, our life's telos. It is only in these reckonings and confrontations that we find a way to be uniquely ourselves, free of the taint of conformity and comfortable, consensual untruths.

Kierkegaard's biographies show us that he attempted this kind of unsparing self-creation in his own tortured life; the choices he made, whether in the domain of personal relationships or in his critiques of conventional stupidities and pieties, significantly determined the kind of life he was able to live.[28] Reading his biographies assures us he was speaking from experience, that he had undergone that which he wrote about and knew whereof he spoke; he had experienced terrible cognitive dissonance and an agonizing reckoning with the irrevocable consequences of his decisions. The highly personal philosophical doctrines he offered us thus speak to our hearts and minds alike; his writing is obscure and elliptical, and yet we press on through its thickets, trusting that we will find rare, glittering, perspicuous insights that illuminate our human predicaments like the best art and literature do. He reveals his enduring torments and encourages us to confront ours; to read Kierkegaard is to be reassured that least of all is philosophy an academic or intellectual exercise; instead, it is what it was supposed to be, a matter of the heart and intellect that finds its proofs in the life it enables us to live.

Kierkegaard uses the term "anxiety" ("angest" in the original Danish) to refer both to a human feeling and to the structure of a human being that gives rise to that feeling;[29] anxiety becomes a constitutive aspect of human existence. What we experience when we are anxious is a fundamental human sensation, often covered up by layers of acculturation, training, education, and ideological programming; this most basic human affect of all, the feeling that tells us we are human, above the breath, the touch, the taste, the vision, is anxiety. But anxiety speaks, too, to an acute sense of isolation in this cosmos, to the possibility that the benevolent hand of God has passed over but missed us, so that we are "forgotten by God, overlooked among the millions and millions in this enormous household."[30]

Kierkegaard's treatment of anxiety is sometimes described as "theological" or "religious" or "spiritual." This is because Kierkegaard finds anxiety in the "possibility of sin" present to man and wants to provide an understanding of the state of mind of primal man (Adam) as he is tempted, by incomplete knowledge, to choose, act, and, therefore, possibly sin. In the often bewilderingly dense and obtuse *Concept of Anxiety*, anxiety is my anticipation of sin, my sense I am about to move beyond the bounds of the current state and act, or experience, or feel; it is "the psychological state of the individual that preceded the fall."[31] The "fall" is, of course, the biblical catastrophe that delivered man from the state of innocent ignorance to sinful knowing, from blissful, guided protection to anxious, unguided pathfinding through a world of possibility and, therefore, sin. Anxiety is "the psychological state" that is "the condition for the possibility of the fall" because "Adam ... is both attracted to the forbidden fruit and repelled from it."[32] His anxiety was not the cause for his original sin; rather, through it, he had the experience of "being able."[33] Anxiety, then, is the normal state of the innocent person where "innocent" means "before acting." Stripped of its theological frills, this language means that we are always anxious before acting, as we contemplate both the possible action and our ability and desire to commit it, tempered by a fear of the uncertain consequences of so acting (and, significantly for our social existence, a fear of whether such an action is approved or condemned—by whatever earthly or unearthly power or expectation: the relationship between anxiety and guilt is acute here—as, we will soon see, it is in Freud's theories of anxiety). The paradigmatic example here is that of the vertigo we suffer as we stand on a cliff's edge; we are fearful not because we are in danger of falling, but because we know we could, if we wanted, jump over the edge to our death. We fear ourselves, and what we are capable of, at this moment.

Kierkegaard considers anxiety an "ambiguous relation"[34] of both an "attraction to and a repulsion from the nothingness of future possibilities";[35] it is the tension between "eagerness and uneasiness,"[36] a "desire for what one fears."[37] In theological terms, man is made uneasy by sin and tempted by it alike; we want and desire the forbidden fruit and all it promises, but we dread the consequences of biting into it. In secular terms, we both desire and fear life, for life is the domain of uncertain experience, of reward and damnation alike. We are driven forward into time, by curiosity and by the desire to know, explore, experience, but we are fearful; this tension between the unrealized future and the possible, and the actual present with its acquisitions, its goods to lose, is human anxiety.

Kierkegaard offers us a pair of piercing formulations that capture essential aspects of anxiety. They reveal too that if anxiety lacks a determinate object, that if it is about "nothing," then that nothing is the future.[38] First, in asking "What is anxiety?" and answering, "It is the next day,"[39] anxiety is revealed as our reaction to the ineluctable uncertainty of the future. As human beings, with our lack of divine omniscience, we do not know; we cannot know. Yet, despite this lack of knowledge, we must press on, into the domain of action and fearful consequence; we must investigate the formless future, which reminds us of our inability to construct and define its contours with precision. We may realize that without divine, inhuman, omniscience, there is no relief from anxiety. More dramatically, Kierkegaard also asserts, "Anxiety is actually nothing but impatience."[40] We are straining at the bit, but afraid to find out what waits for us. We want to live but are afraid of experiencing life; *we want life but are afraid of living*. This is the tension that Kierkegaard finds in anxiety; it is present in the movement from possibility to actuality, from the present to the future, from ambiguous desire to concrete, committing, action. (These formulations also bring Kierkegaard's notions closer to Buddhism, for dukkha is the feeling that the present moment is tainted by anticipation of future loss, and social and moral transgression. Indeed, Kierkegaard insists that even in "good fortune's most hidden recesses of happiness, there dwells also the dread that is despair,"[41] another point of commonality with dukkha.)

For Kierkegaard, man is a curious admixture of the material and the spiritual, an artful combination of the physical and psychical, of body and mind, of "future and past, possibility and necessity, finitude and infinitude."[42] These polarities, of which we are dimly aware when we reckon with the complexity of our worldly experiences and our ambivalent responses to them, are "united by spirit,"[43] our awareness of our possibility for sinning, which underwrites the anxious relationship of our provisional, under-construction and as-yet-unmade self to its unspecified future possibilities. If we were purely physical, empirical creatures, we would be constrained and hemmed in by empirical reality and physical laws; but as admixtures of body and soul, we are rendered free by the presence of spirit, which elevates us out of the mundane realm of the physical through a painful and terrifying awareness that we are not determined creatures. But we are not just creatures who are free to act; *we are creatures who are aware we are free to act*; we could have been creatures who are free to choose but are not conscious of their freedom. A purely physical, empirical, material being, one regulated by the laws of nature, would not possess this self-consciousness of spirit, which reminds us we are capable of sin, of making choices between good and evil, and bringing both good and evil on ourselves. Our freedom is possibility itself, the spiritual, nonmaterial, and nonempirical aspect of man that is unrealized and awaits completion. Anxiety is how freedom is made actual by indicating to us that possibility in our lives is possible: we are those creatures who are seduced, entranced, and finally galvanized into action by an awareness of possibility, a state suffused with anxiety.

Anxiety, Kierkegaard suggested, in keeping with his spiritual concerns, is what we experience as we move from innocence to knowledge; it is a premonition of the task that awaits us, an intimation in our lives of our inner selves, and a beckoning toward what we might be. Much as a mountaineer feels a tremor of anticipatory fear as she confronts an icy, steep traverse across a chasm, but presses on, knowing that turning back is not an option, that stern, rewarding, indispensable self-examination awaits ahead, we must, too, take that first step and move on. Anxiety becomes the road we must travel on from a state of anticipation to realization; those who turn back from it, who forgo the journey, remain static and neurotically confined.

As we move onward on our paths of self-creation,[44] actualizing some of our possibilities, our psychic, moral, and intellectual growth involves defiance of, and resistance to, established norms and procedures (these may be familial, social, or religious); our self is unique and must find a unique realization, chosen by us. The trusted path is secure; the path of perpetual creation is not. Societal and familial conflict and crises confront us in our developmental trajectories as we find ourselves threatened by spiritual and social isolation; selfhood is gained by confronting the anxiety—and guilt—inherent in taking a stand against one's environment. Kierkegaard suggests that willing to become oneself is our true calling in this world, the task we were born to accomplish, for he, like Nietzsche, imagined us artists, bringing a work of art, our evolving self, into being with our actions.[45] This means, too, that for Kierkegaard, the world's diversions, which call us to achieve socially respectable standards of income or status, are pernicious diversions from our existential task of self-creation. At the very least, if you find yourself meeting such social norms, and being declared a worldly success, you should be deeply suspicious of what you have in fact achieved. Conversely, failure to achieve such standards is, at the least, cause not for irredeemable despair, but instead for a searching examination into what truly motivates and moves us.

Our choices are destructive of an older life; what awaits is an unknown entity, our new self and life. Our self-creation entails that there is no predetermined self waiting to be realized; rather it can take shape only gradually and, much like a slowly developing Polaroid, might horrify us by what it reveals, so might our emerging self. We may try to avoid this responsibility for what we make of ourselves by trying to become someone else, perhaps an imagined ideal, a traditional and conventional one visible in the actions of others. Those pathways lead to "despair," a state in which we are, consciously or not, unwilling to be ourselves. This is a state of true spiritual sickness, a "sickness unto death" as it were.[46]

Kierkegaard considered the crucial aspect of our distinctive human consciousness to be not merely perceptual and sensory awareness, our much-vaunted phenomenal consciousness, but rather an acute awareness of an inner world of volition and choice, the presence of spirit. The more heightened this awareness of possibility, the greater our degree of self-attainment; we become more realized the more conscious we are of ourselves as the loci of action and choice.[47] Within ourselves, acute psychic conflicts are engendered by our inability to confront anxiety, the signature of our freedom, and move through and on; we need to let anxiety flow though our being, so that our growth is not impeded. The postponed or repressed conflict with authority or an older life plan, a crisis in relationships, postponements of decisions, situations requiring the assumption of responsibility, moments of isolation, thoughts of death: these knots in our being require patient unraveling in the here and now, not escapes to the to-be-realized future. As we will see, these suggestions of unresolved psychic conflicts bring Kierkegaard into consonance with psychoanalytic claims that repressed mental states require "working through," for they will otherwise manifest themselves in neurotic symptoms. Anxiety indicates the presence of a problematic, an inner conflict requiring *a decision, a choice, an action* to resolve.

Anxiety appears, too, as we seek independence and freedom even as we crave the safety we seek to leave behind. Many of our rebellions, putative experiments to test the waters outside the security of the home, remain at the level of empty gestures as we scurry back to safety at the first hint of a threat; as distraught and amused parents alike notice, children flee from conformity with their family into the arms of the conformity of their peer groups, there to dress up and behave like every other member of that group. Anxiety thus generates tremendous dissonance, for we both crave and shrink from freedom; it is "a desire for what one dreads."[48] We experience this dissonance always, for we wish to both actualize and negate our possibilities—in each case, we can see that an undetermined outcome awaits. "Life decisions," like moving, changing jobs, divorce, committing to personal relationships, changing college majors, *must*, then, trigger anxiety. For Kierkegaard, the difference between neurotic and healthy individuals is marked by their responses to anxiety: the healthy individual moves ahead despite the inner conflict and anxiety, actualizing her freedom, whereas the unhealthy retreat to a safer enclosure, sacrificing their freedom as they do so.

Anxiety's presence indicates the heartening and yet terrifying possibility of a distinctively fashioned, unique life, which requires the destruction of older modes of being.[49] Guilt is thus anxiety's inevitable companion; a therapeutically revealing maneuver is to investigate whether our feelings of anxiety are inextricably linked with feelings of guilt; if they are, it is worth asking, "What do we feel guilty of doing or not doing? *Who or what do we imagine we are answerable to for this failure?*" The answers we might find are both revealing and enlightening. (Notice, too, a relationship here with the Freudian analysis to follow: We are anxious because we feel we will be found guilty of a social or moral sin, or evil; hence we repress our desires, our feelings; if it is dangerous to express our anger at a loved one, that is, if we sense it is "wrong," then the feeling of that anger arising within us causes us anxiety. We are made anxious by our emotions, by our desires and needs, for we relentlessly moralize them, asking whether these are appropriate or correct; this searching moral self-examination, as we had noted Nietzsche suggested, could be productive of a guilt-stricken, anxiety-ridden "bad conscience.") Those who create do not shy away from anxiety and guilt, rather they navigate it and move through it.[50] We understand "moving through" by analogy to swimming: We do not swim against the current; we do not try to swim to shore; we move ahead with the flow, sustaining the terrifying feeling of turbulence, of a loss of control, of no solid bottom for our feet, which must continue to kick. We cannot proceed anyway else; the tug of the current is terrifying, but if we fight it, or do not take any action at all, we will drown.

We may give up our precious freedom, our intimation of possibility and spirit, by indulging in neurotic reactions to anxiety, fatally restricting an essential development by blocking paths to maturity and self-realization.[51] We may avoid anxiety in this "cowardly age" in which "by way of diversions" the "torches, yells and cymbals"[52] of yore have been replaced by television, social media, and endless updates and notifications. Kierkegaard therefore explicitly valorizes the "ethical individual"[53] who denies themselves any kind of palliatives, whether psychic, intellectual, or pharmaceutical, for in treating ourselves to comforting illusions, we are living an untruth and enslaving ourselves.[54] This evasion of anxiety means we lose a precious opportunity to produce a unique synthesis of body and spirit: not animal, not God, not inanimate matter. Beasts and angels have a well-defined being; they can be no other—their behavior is defined and known. But we can be beast and angel alike to ourselves and to those we love.

Our distinctive anxiety is engendered by our understanding of the dimensions of possibility, which is more frightening than actuality. The realized world is limited; the possible world is not. The realized world is limited by human actions and physical laws; the possible future and the afterworld, the afterlife, are unlimited in their scope. There, we see beauty and terror; we see threat and promise; we see heaven and hell; all is visible within the space of possibility. The more we imagine, the more spaces of possibility we conjure up, the more creative our assessments of choices and actions, the greater the anxiety we feel. Ironically, the more creative we are in our fashioning of our lives and ourselves, the more anxiety we commit ourselves to; the creative person is supremely gifted in their capacity to summon up alternate states of reality; among these lurk terrifying possibilities.

And it is only when we travel through the anxiety of possibility that we find the courage to encounter the fear of actuality. Such a journey of edification requires accepting our human condition, "that absolutely nothing can be demanded of life, and that horror, perdition, and annihilation, live next door to every human being";[55] we must learn "that every anxiety for which [we feel] alarm can come upon [us] the very next instant."[56] This education by "possibility," "the most difficult of all categories," allows us to grasp the "terrifying just as well as the smiling."[57] To do so is to realize that life's possibilities are not bounded, save by logic and conceptual imagination. Monsters lurk here, as do angels; here indeed be dragons. There are no boundaries beyond which the terrible cannot advance, no wall that can hold it back; there is no specified interval for joys to last; they may be as fleeting and ephemeral as the lightest of our quicksilver fancies. To be truly educated by this knowledge, by the journey here, one must plumb life's beckoning depths, and soar into and above its intimated heights. Here anxieties acquire shape and form, crystallizing into fears; here, within the space of possibility, as we look around at its curling edges, we see abysses lurking—these indicate the limits of our imagination, beyond which monsters worse than the ones our minds have been able to conjure up find their abode. To retreat from this feverishly imagined space into that of actuality, the lived empirical life, "reality" as we call it, is to arrive suitably chastened by the realization that we had ever dared demand from this world any consolation whatsoever; we learn to give thanks for the spaces of possibility that have been realized in our lives to our favor. This actual, realized world, for all its terrors, is still less onerous than the world whose contours we had so vividly and powerfully sketched as we traversed the spaces of possibility. The closer we look possibility in the face, the more of a home we find in actuality, which for all its terrors is only a subset of the possible.[58]

For a *Christian* existentialist like Kierkegaard, faith, committed and sincere, rescues us from anxiety; conversely, anxiety points in the direction of faith, for faith "extricates itself from anxiety's moment of death."[59] Kierkegaard imagined that the answer to existential absurdity was a commitment to belief in Christ—not the conventional one of the church, but rather the unique divine individual, the only "true Christian"—and considered our recognition of anxiety to be the signal for us to seek out faith. Those who do will find that "anxiety becomes . . . a ministering spirit that leads him, against its will, where he will."[60] This anxiety is not a demon then, but a spiritual force within us, a reminder of our distinctive, spirit-infused humanity. Kierkegaard suggests that the deepest fortitude, the greatest source of personal strength, the greatest commitment to the certainty of faith, deliverance, and hope, develops out of an individual's successful confrontations with anxiety-creating experiences, on their way to a matured self. Indeed, as *The Concept of Anxiety* concludes, Kierkegaard proclaims, "Whoever has learned to be anxious in the right way has learned the ultimate."[61] If we have truly comprehended the significance of anxiety in our lives and its relationship to our spiritual deliverance, then we have put this world's empirical worries in perspective; we have learned this world's (guilt-inducing) demands carry little importance compared to our awesome existential responsibility to be ourselves. If, as Kierkegaard insisted, courage comes about only when a greater fear chases out a lesser fear,[62] then we will find the wherewithal for confronting anxiety when we are fully cognizant of the terrible cost of not doing so.

Kierkegaard was not oblivious to the historical and cultural location of humans that resulted in their idiosyncratic encounters with anxiety, for he considered that in different societal structures, anxiety takes different forms;[63] individuals exist within "an historical nexus,"[64] so the intensity of our anxiety depends on a highly specific environment characterized by "particular cultural circumstances."[65] In some societies there is no emphasis on self-construction; its members have no idea that they are anxious because there is "no conscious relation to the future"; in yet others, "the future is viewed as fated."[66] Catholics, equipped with a different notion of faith, the soul, and the presence of spirit, are anxious in a different way than Hindus or Jews or Buddhists are, with their diverse cosmologies, metaphysics, and normative sensibilities; or than Americans in the twentieth century, or Chinese in the nineteenth century, who lived in widely varying empirical circumstances. Still, even though the environment conditions the individual and intensifies anxiety by giving its object a more concrete form as the nothing of anxiety is made into a something, the environment never wholly determines the individual. Put in this fashion, Kierkegaard acknowledges the materiality present in our lives while still placing the existential responsibility for self-construction on the individual.

It is crucial, then, that we understand we are the fount of anxiety, for it is not produced from without; it is relentless and acts from within;[67] no matter where we turn or look, we find "anxiety is there."[68] Procrastination is an exemplary example: we seek relief from the anxiety engendered by the task before us by fleeing into the arms of a greater anxiety caused by the noncompletion of the task we have fled from. But, considering Kierkegaard's typically perspicuous claim that our courage to face a particular kind of fear comes about only when we face an even greater fear, the procrastinating writer finally gets to work when the wrath of the editor, or the loss of the reader or her own artistic sensibility, strikes her as a greater fear than the anxieties of the blank page and her fumbling attempts to fill it.

The most significant aspect of Kierkegaard's suggestion that we pay attention to anxiety is that by our noticing it, talking about it, and acknowledging it, not as pathology, but as an informative part of ourselves, it becomes not something to be expelled, but to be welcomed as a *message* from ourselves. To stay with anxiety, to stop and respond to its challenge, is to accept a form of secular communion with ourselves. There is thus a Nietzschean note in Kierkegaard's injunctions: we must display *amor fati*, a love of fate; we must own our anxiety as part of us, integrated and deployed to make our lives what we wish them to be. Kierkegaard, then, urges us to not withdraw from experiencing our anxiety, for what if we live our lives around not wanting to experience anxiety? We would then experience true despair according to Kierkegaard; we would have been in anxiety, but we would not have listened to it, not tried to understand it—and therefore not understood ourselves or who we could be. We would have had our only chance to be ourselves and yet have disdained it. For Kierkegaard, to regard anxiety as a pathology leads to regarding ourselves as pathology, to understanding our lives as problems, not opportunities; it is "a prosaic stupidity" that would "think of it as a disorder."[69]

Kierkegaard and Nietzsche, in anticipating psychoanalysis, find a conceptual relationship between guilt and anxiety; very often when we are anxious, we are stricken by guilt. Are we committing transgressions, real or imagined, against some order, moral, religious, or social, imposed on us? Are we apprehensive over the prospects of condemnation or excommunication that awaits if we commit or omit some acts? Who or what do we imagine is placed in a position to be able to so judge us? Where do their evaluative scales come from? Who are their architects? That voice in our head, the one that castigates us, whose hectoring we shrink from and dread: whose is it? To investigate such queries is to do no less than to uncover the structure of beliefs and affects that constitute our self-in-the-making. Kierkegaard's greatest blessing to the anxious is that he assures us that the mundane business of living our lives is a matter of supreme importance; the anxiety that afflicts us, and speaks to us to in doing so, is not a stranger, but ourselves. The hallowing and sanctification of the weekday with the ultimate, the task of confronting and working our anxiety on our way to being ourselves, is to be regarded not as a burden, but as an opportunity to be seized.

The Courage to Be

The existentialist philosopher and Protestant (Lutheran) theologian Paul Tillich wrote his classic work *The Courage to Be* to claim that we need a distinctive courage to exist, to persist in living, to just "be." Tillich's book is not titled *The Courage to Wage War* or *The Courage to Climb Mountains*; we are heroes, courageous ones, if we can affirm life and its singular challenge: anxiety. In displaying the "democratic" courage of Socrates, who in freely affirming his own death, affirmed life,[70] we rely on an acute, hard-earned wisdom about the nature of our being: it is suffused with an awareness of its own nonexistence. We do not have to fight wars to face death; we face it every day we decide to go on living. This existential anxiety is not amenable to medication; so long as we are aware of the nature of our existence, we are made anxious. The descriptions Tillich offers of this species of anxiety are suggestive; they help us understand why some kinds of anxiety feel the way they do, and why they are ever present, unshakeable, a perennial companion to every waking hour, a permanent underwriter of the most ordinary of apprehensions. Tillich thus successfully captures the *mood* of anxiety; it is not a concrete, tangible fear, but a chill that runs through my being as it becomes aware of itself, its nature. To not be so anxious, we would have to be unconscious or dead.

In Tillich's understanding of anxiety, it is a pointer to a realm that, though not of this world, is ever present in it: our certain death and eventual unknowable nothingness. Anxiety is a peculiar awareness of the "nonbeing" that awaits after death:[71] a subterranean ever presence, an unshakeable shadow, the basement of our moods and emotions. This existential anxiety is constitutive of human consciousness; man may be defined as the being whose consciousness is characterized by its perpetual awareness of its own extinction, its being limited by a void so profound that intellectual concepts break down in reckoning with it. Our life is a moment of existence surrounded by nonexistence, before, after, and all around; and we know it, through our persistent confrontation with the threat of "nonbeing"[72] and its "naked anxiety."[73] This darkness that intrudes into every image of clarity, this dark lining of every silver cloud, which underwrites the unease of even satiation, contentment, or pleasure: this is anxiety. Courage is our affirmation of life, of continued existence in the face of this certain condemnation to perpetual nonbeing, our resolutely holding fast in the face of the nonexistence that death promises. We live on, acting and choosing, with nothingness and death as companions, a demonstration of not exceptional, but ordinary courage, which is not any less remarkable for what it requires.

As Tillich understands it, life's varied eventualities and disasters do not cause anxiety directly, rather it is their provocation of the "latent awareness"[74] of our death, our nonbeing, that does; a mundane concrete fear, a routine crisis—a missed payment, a financial crisis, a delayed phone call from a lover, a bad grade on a minor exam, an angry look from an important friend—reaches into our consciousness to aggravate this formless anxiety over the associated possibility, no matter how remote, of death and nothingness. Even when no danger is apparent, the fact of being, of existing, of being conscious and awake, can remind us this is not destined to last forever. Anxiety is an intimation that our lives are limited, as are our powers and capacities; that though within us lie multitudes, and around us are bounties unlimited of natural beauty and man-made wealth, we are finite creatures. We are profoundly aware our lives are ripples in a cosmic pond, that an infinite cosmos will endure and persist while we pass on to unbounded nothingness. Anxiety is a reminder of our curious state of being, dangling between two formless infinities; though we are finite, we participate in terrifying incursions into infinity.

Our awareness that we could be nonexistent is distinctive, for this awareness is not just of "death," a term invested with ample cultural meaning and affect, but of literally nothing. Our knowledge of nonbeing is therefore not an abstract formulation committed to memory; rather nothingness is a persistent companion, a presence that is the crucial determinant of an unease that always accompanies us, through darkness and light, through happiness and sorrow, through the uncertain trajectories of earthly fortunes. What makes our anxiety intractable is that it has no identifiable object and indeed cannot; anxiety is a fear of that unknown that is unknowable. This "naked anxiety"[75] about nonbeing is unbearable in its horror; it is a nauseating, terrifying experience, rendering gibbering fools of the bravest. Because anxiety lacks a focal point, because its centrality is an effacement of being, a wiping out of all that exists, we cannot engage or struggle with it; our nothingness is "not a possible object of fear and courage."[76] Such anxiety "belongs to existence itself";[77] distractions and diversions and medications are futile; we must find a way to live with this anxiety.

To understand the mood of anxiety as Tillich formulates it, consider it a state of consciousness in which we sense an interloper, an intruder, squatting on our mental domain, forcing us to acknowledge its presence. This "fingerprint of nothingness" as it were, cannot be given a face or a form; it cannot be stared down, for there is nothing to look at; it cannot be seized, for there is nothing tangible to capture. This enduring agony of a formless and shapeless anxiety is experienced by a being who experiences death while still alive, who experiences an existence suffused with its own termination, its own negation; anxiety intimates what lies beyond, formless and forbidding. Nothingness in the presence of being is the shadow in the light, a reminder of the eventual effacing of the light's brilliance and illumination. To step into that shadow is to feel an uneasy chill, much like how mountaineers experience the sun passing behind a cloud, dropping down beneath the valley rim, casting a radiant alpine cirque and meadow into a threatening dusk.

Nonexistence, then, is the *fons et origo* of anxiety; the most mundane of everyday facts is tinged with this intimation of our destined nothingness. When we are absent, voluntarily or not, from a social situation, we are reminded that there was a time when we were absent in this world and that there will be another when we will be so in the future (every shared photograph on social media that does not include us nudges our awareness in this direction); our lovers remind us there was a time when we did not exist in their lives, and did not matter in their reckonings (think of the crippling melancholia that afflicts us when we look at a photograph of our lovers before they met us); our children are aware there was a time when they did not exist in their parents' lives (and they will eventually become aware their parents will not last forever); parents are aware they will not be alive while their children and friends and family live on. Through anxiety, then, we are reminded of our transience, our fragile, contingent, unstable presence in this world. We can be rid of this anxiety only if we were not mortal, something other than what we are.

For Tillich, anxiety takes three forms, indexed by the ways nothingness threatens our meaningful existence, our spirituality, our very being: the anxieties of "fate and death"; the anxieties of "emptiness and loss of meaning"; and the anxieties of "guilt and condemnation."[78] These "inescapable" forms of anxiety,[79] the inevitable companions of a being concerned with redeeming itself, with doing justice to its sense that its life is but a partial signature of its existence, concretely manifest themselves in gnawing, nagging questions that dog our every station: What will happen to me in the future? When will I die? How will I die? What will happen to me when I die? Will I suffer for a long time? Will my loved ones suffer when they see me suffer? What will happen to all that I leave behind, my family, my friends, my loves, my works? What if I live my life in the wrong way and waste it? What if I do not live my life richly enough and do not take sufficient advantage of it? Why do I not feel fulfilled despite doing all my resident cultures and ideologies demand of me? What awaits me once I have fulfilled my life's "assigned" tasks? What will be my reward for having done what was expected of me? Have I made the wrong decisions and am now fated to eternal perdition? Have I been a good person? All work cannot be completed, and neither can it survive; why, then, am I expected to dedicate my life to it? These questions remain unanswered as we live our lives; answers without theistic foundations, without promises of an afterlife, do not comfort us, for we sense other humans cover up their own anxieties in providing assurances to us; they are as uncertain and terrified as we are, their confidence mere self-protective bluster. Every existential question raised above becomes a confrontation with anxiety, each requiring an affirmation of continued existence in the absence of definitive answers, a blow struck against our nonbeing, our extinguishing.[80]

Such intimations of nonbeing are not merely a burden. Anxiety can be understood as a life-sustaining force too, as nonbeing "forces [being] to affirm itself dynamically";[81] it drives us onward to ask, to seek, to inquire, to clarify, to verify, to confirm, to reduce our uncertainty, to secure reassurances about our chosen paths; our great distractions and diversions, our life's affairs, generate the material world and its preoccupations, all deliverances from our anxiety. The gods looking down on us from their lofty perches should be impressed by the sheer fecundity of thought and the richness of action with which we combat our anxiety by generating those mental and physical distractions we call our lives' tasks.

Tillich's analysis of anxiety is an acute reminder of how perplexing and terrifying we find death and our resultant postmortem state. We are told God and religious doctrines of the immortality of the soul exist because we fear death, so we laugh at the religious while we down our stiff drinks, pop our many pills, switch channels, check for "Likes" and "Retweets" relentlessly, and work sixteen-hour days into exhausted, insensate oblivion. Tillich denies that such desperate maneuvers evade existential anxiety, for we, as biological creatures, are keenly aware our biological termination is also the termination of our self.[82] So we insist we will accept death when it comes even as we reveal with our actions and our nervous, frantic preoccupations that we do not accept it now and will not accept it when it does come.

As children, we found death early in life; we sensed, however dimly, the fate of all things and beings, an intuitive knowledge confirmed by the lives we subsequently live. Dying and death are of this world; we see deaths on television; we see friends and family members die; we bear witness to the pain of cancer patients, the convulsions of heart attacks, the mangled bodies of strangers lying on the side of the highway; we dread a similar fate. But though death is certain, its manner, nature, and time is not. This is a great, anxiety-provoking uncertainty. And knowledge of the manner, nature, and time of death provokes anxiety too, for we suffer an anxiety associated with not knowing how we will react when we are dying. I know I will suffer pain; what I dread are my reactions to its unspecified nature. Our fear is directed at the particulars of death while our anxiety is rooted in uncertainty over our response to death; we are anxious in the face of death because we bear anticipatory fear toward the pain and decrepitude that stalks those destined for death. We are fearful of being fearful, scared of being scared.

Death, the end point of this life, can be feared; we are anxious about what comes after our body is consigned to the flames or lowered into the ground. We realize it is not death that threatens us as much as nothingness; what we fear most are those dark nights when we will wake, and unable to sleep, contemplate in quiet horror the mystery that awaits after death. We can only vaguely sense what lies after death; we struggle to imagine the unimaginable, the negation of our everyday being, which is characterized by presence and persistence. When we are anxious, we anticipate our reactions to the threat that some object poses to us; our fear of these anticipated reactions is our anxiety.[83] But what is the nature of our fear about something, our postmortem nothingness, that is inconceivable?

That eternally indecisive Danish prince, Hamlet, wondered too: "What dreams may come after / When we have shuffled off this mortal coil / Must give us pause" and that "The dread of something after death / The undiscovered country, from whose bourn / No traveler returns, puzzles the will."[84] The materialistically minded reassure themselves oblivion awaits, a blankness and a void like the sleep we enjoyed before we were ejected into the world naked, helpless, and conscious; they reassure themselves it will be dreamless. Others—convinced by the world's great religions—speculate eternal torment or pleasures lie in store. Yet others worry that states of being we have no conception of are our postmortem fate; they are the most susceptible to anxiety about the afterlife as they suspect the ostensibly certain have hidden their uncertainty, an invitation to Hamlet's anxiety, particularly well. For all, death and its associated nothingness are terrifying because it is the wrong kind of immortality. We came from the eternal void, delivered to this brief respite; we dread a return to that same endlessness after we have experienced the consciousness of this existence. We do not want immortality of the wrong kind, like agony in hellfire, or a lonely tenure in a dark place. Our anxiety is a reminder, no matter how artfully concealed in our consciousness by humdrum daily life, that immortality of an undefined, unknowable kind awaits us.[85]

Tillich's claim that weekday anxiety bottoms out into death anxiety, into the great unknown of death and nothingness, is edifying and suggestive; it helps us understand why mundane losses acquire the terrifying significance they do. A minor material or worldly loss, if symbolically cast and understood as the greatest loss of all, can remind us of our own effacement. The notion that our latent awareness of nothingness is anxiety indicates why anxiety is always present no matter what our worldly state. It accurately reflects a brute fact of existence: the worldly power we gain is hapless in the face of our eventual nothingness, a constraint of which we are always aware, no matter how glibly we seek to render ourselves unaware of it. Indeed, Tillich's analysis suggests that *our fear of nothingness is the "fear that underlies all fears," the bottoming out of all named variants of anxiety.* And so is death anxiety; if we were to pursue the roots of one of our high-level fears, down to its subterranean origins, what kind of fear would we find lurking there? A salutary therapeutic intervention directed at oneself is to ask ourselves why some distinctive fear or worry is quite as acute as it is; what other fear is lurking behind it? And behind that? Will we find fears of death and mortality resident there? Perhaps our fears about job security, about making the wrong career choice, bottom out in the fear that we will end up suffering painfully and dying from an untreated disease because we are too indigent to afford medical care—an exemplary instance of how a tangible material fear, remote from existential considerations, finds its foundation in a formless death anxiety.

The philosophical acceptance of death and our eventual nothingness that Tillich urges us toward entails the acceptance of several existential axioms, each generating and sustaining an acute anxiety: the finitude of our lives; the finality and irrevocability of our death; the certainty of the end of one's life; the continued persistence of the world and its affairs beyond us, indifferent and undisturbed; our utter ordinariness as we take our place in line; the monstrous indifference of the uncaring cosmos to our life plans; and our conscious awareness of these constraints. Life-affirming, courageous acts like those required to live life every day require us to integrate these axioms into our understanding of ourselves, to face the possibility of death squarely, and to bring death closer to us, not more distant. Which we do, of course, when we choose to go on living; we bring death closer every second of every hour, every day. Tillich's analysis reminds us, too, that an important determinant of dealing with anxiety is to realize the braveries we have already demonstrated our capacity for; we must package those understandings of ourselves into our self-conception; we must erect ourselves as heroes in our minds for getting up in the morning and turning our face toward the rising sun, to welcome another day of uncertainty and doubt, and yes, anxiety.

The ever presence of death and nothingness, and the reminders it provides us that the world we live in is mere contingency, is the dramatic grounding of the mood of anxiety we find in another existentialist philosopher, the controversial and polarizing Martin Heidegger.

The Uncanny Mood of Anxiety

Reading Martin Heidegger on anxiety[86] may make you more anxious, not less, not just because the difficulty of his philosophical prose is intimidating and oppressive, but also because the picture he paints of human existence is as stark and uncompromising as it is. I first tried to read Heidegger almost three decades ago; I often learn more from those who write about Heidegger than from the man himself.[87] Disdain for his dense and obscure writing style permits some academics to use his now-unquestioned Nazism—visible in his many pronouncements, writings, and actions, before and during Germany's darkest hours—to decline to read him. I sympathize with these stylistic and substantive rejections; yet there are acute insights to be found in Heidegger's works, of great value in understanding a particular species of anxiety.

For Heidegger, the bare facts of human existence—which takes place in time and cannot be considered apart from it—are death (the certainty that *awaits* us), nothingness (the unknowable state *after* death), and "thrownness," meaning a presence in an *already* constructed and prepared state where we find ourselves as we become self-conscious; these represent the hard, nonnegotiable constraints that make life meaningful; their resolute acceptance, not denial, is the only path toward an authentic existence. The mood that enables us to come to grips with, and realize the significance of, this crucial trifecta of existential parameters is anxiety.

Heidegger's evidence for his philosophical claims is an invitation to withdraw from the given, the ordinary, the normal, and to pay attention to our perennial companions, our moods and affects, which we trust as revealing and noetic; we do not privilege logical thought or reasoning. Our moods allow us to discover those things that really matter about, and the true nature of, existence; these moods—those of melancholia, restlessness, unease, fear, discontent—conceal and disclose the nature of existence partially and yet in deeply significant ways. These private reveries of the experienced and felt—and not reasoned theory, which is formalized and stated in terms distancing us from the bareness of existence, of the fact of Being—are the golden road to a deeper understanding of ourselves. We gain the most perspicuous kind of self-awareness through our experience of *angst*; anxiety allows us to understand the nature of being, our relationship to existence, by exploring the mood or affect that accompanies it.[88] Heidegger makes anxiety essential; without an encounter with it we have no chance of our understanding or approaching our "selfhood" or an authentic relationship with our freedom and a life free of illusion.

Heidegger's reliance on the moods of human beings, and not on an abstract Universal Reason divorced from the concrete particulars of our lived experiences, is crucially significant, for he urges us to pay attention to the idiosyncrasies of the ways in which we feel and relate to our being in this world, not the ways we are instructed to feel by conventionally established forms of thought. Heidegger therefore urges us to step away from the socially constructed notion of *Das Man* ("everyman")—a generic entity that represents social conformity, and that offers us the reassurance of a comforting home amid the world's strangeness. Anxiety is the realization that this abode is put together, a house of cards depending for its stability on the mutual agreement and the sympathetic coordination of the utter strangers who are our fellow travelers. Our home is afflicted by a memorable fragility; once we have experienced its resultant anxiety, we will not forget it quickly, and the possibility we might find ourselves in the same situation never goes away; it is our companion in life.

Anxieties and its moods introduce a new unconventional mode of thinking; within it, the familiarity of the world vanishes, and we are confronted with the sheer contingency of the manmade world.[89] This abnormal world is more revealing than the normal: here, anxiety brings us, our fundamental being, our naked existence, before its own potential, what it is, and what it could be. In our daily lives, we live in an inauthentic mode, awaiting deliverance and salvation from elsewhere; we accept the world as it is constructed (by those before us, complete with their self-serving, power-propagating values and norms), thus abdicating our existential responsibility in furthering it. This kind of existence is superficial; we exist on its surface without a deeper realization of its nature. Here, we are tranquilized and sated; we are not curious; we are not concerned with the nature of existence, our role in it, or our possibilities; we notice the disjuncture of the external world with the internal feeling of our being but pay no heed. Here, we are oblivious to our uniqueness, our peculiarity, and our possibilities; there is a frightening chance we might be born, live, and die without having realized what "this" was all about.[90] But existence leaks through as anxiety "rescues" us. It delivers us not to a mode of existence in which we are merely passively impacted by the world as things or objects are, but rather to one in which we make it by choosing and acting. We start this process by being brought to face existence through a special, distinctive mood that reveals it to us: anxiety.

Heidegger uses the term "uncanny" ("not at home") to refer to our state when we lose the sense this world is a familiar place. When we are immersed in our everyday world, estranged from our existential self and situation, using the handed-down inheritance of the world we were born into, we are in an "everyday" or "fallen" state; as this lapsarian language implies, this is not a state of grace, it is a put-up job, a cover-up, a sweeping under the rug. Anxiety is the prompt for us to cease our absorption in this world of empirical appearance. We are not at home here, a fact we realize as the complacent sense of "being-in-this-world" gives way to an angst-ridden "not-at-home"; we become strangers or outsiders in a formerly understood place. This mood of anxiety, untouched by human affairs, brings us in the presence of the great void of existence and allows us a measure of comprehension of its two central facets: death and nothingness—the former indicating its eventual and certain ending, and the latter indicating that this world, without human choice and action, utterly lacks sense, meaning, and purpose.

Any breakdown of the given ordinary can expose us to the crisis of meaning that an encounter with anxiety produces.

When an everyday tool—like a hammer—with a prescribed function and placement in our economy of life functions as intended, all is well; these objects in the world are "ready-to-hand," present for us, who are "thrown" into the world's situations. Here they are, suffused with the constructed meanings of history and social arrangement; our relationship to them is clear, the actions and choices we must take specified. I must walk to my desk; I must sit down; I must pick up my tools, whose use is defined by their fit with empirical circumstances; I must get to work. But when we are anxious, we become aware of the constructed systems that maintain such a tool; its purpose and its orientation is revealed as contingent and not essential. Now, these objects simply stare blankly back at us; they have lost their imputed meanings and cannot communicate with us anymore. We see them without the layers of meanings conferred on them by us as the world in which I exist has sunk into insignificance. We find ourselves face to face with the sheer blankness—the sheer nothingness—of the world's slate, wiped clean of human meaning, awaiting inscription by us.

This breakdown of the normal causes us to inspect the world anew; we do not feel at home anymore; comfort and safety are lost; we are cast adrift; we undergo an uncanny experience as we realize we are not-at-home. (The similarity of this experience to those so-called psychotic breakdowns, which result in trips to the emergency room and the prescription of psychiatric medication should be noted.) Now, when the fabricated world of artifacts and predetermined meaning crumbles, we experience true existential isolation and dread. Now, as we take a step back from the ordinary, the settled, the established, the normal, we notice how strange, how contingent all "this" is. Now, when we notice our conventional world has broken down or lost its sheen of normalcy, our anxiety, hidden and buried under layers of conformity and psychological defense mechanisms, appears as a state of extreme, terrifying disorientation; the undefined and undifferentiated world does not make sense anymore. In Sartre's famous and forbiddingly difficult novel *Nausea*, the world is revealed to its central character, Roquentin, as "uncanny" when its sheer, naked, nauseating being becomes visible upon his viewing of the roots of a tree in a garden. The vision of a tree in the park and its roots induce in Roquentin an acute awareness that the known world he inhabits gives out at a certain point, and he is left to flounder in its primal, basic being, without meaning conferred on it via agreement with fellow humans.

Here in this state, a frightening series of thoughts that reckon with the contingency of my constructed world confront me: Who am I? My name? Given to me by my parents; I could have had many others. My nationality? A contingent accident generated by the vicissitudes of my parents' lives. My nation? A historical accident that came into being only a few centuries ago. My religion? I could have had another faith, been brought up to believe in other gods. My language, the one in which I express my deepest thoughts? The result of my being programmed to speak a local dialect depending on my cultural location and my family's history; I could have been thinking, writing, and speaking in another. My best friends? Utter strangers, who know me through a series of fortuitous circumstances. My children? Strangers too, brought into this world by me, who have taken shape before my eyes, who consider me an enduring mystery, and who will remain mysteries themselves. My parents? Historical accidents, bumblers pretending to know all, their lives and motivations destined to remain hidden from me, their origin and identity a great perplexity. Those great priests and sages and philosophers and writers, supposed authoritative guides for my life? "Human, all too human," subject to these same contingencies and fragilities. What, then, of the great certainty that those great systems of thought—religion or philosophy or political ideology—promise us? A structure of seeming fixity, in truth a house of cards, put together and guaranteed by other tormented and frail human beings. All we hold dear and fixed is accidental, the result of coincidences and flukes; the solidity of the world is a careful contrivance by other humans, ignorant and anxious, just like me. The foundations of our world and existence are built on sand. We are bags of blood, bone, and flesh, our consciousness and life a historical accident. What then of us? Who are we, really? What is my real name? What is this all about? When this surface, this sheen of the normal, is removed, what and who am I?

Suddenly, I am cold and scared, and I reach out for someone to comfort me to tell me all will be well; I flee back to safety, to definition, to the known and fixed and secure and unchanging, the bosom of the constructed world; we seek a return to the normal, for we do not wish to find the world anew. There is a way I am conditioned to be by the world; it is a place of safety and refuge. I always find my way back there, there to take on socially assumed and assigned roles and responsibilities, to find the ready-made life awaiting. In this world, I have a name, a nationality, a religion, and codes of conduct; I have been told where to go, what to do; my systems of means and ends are clearly marked out; my predetermined roles are open for me, inviting me with their safety, definition, and certainty, and bringing in their train, their ever-demanding normative and performative constraints that oppress me and make me anxious. It is tempting to let ourselves become part of this constructed world, where when we open our eyes, we find ourselves "thrown" into a situation with acts, responsibilities, and choices laid out for us.

But that glimpse of wonder and terror, that terrified and nauseated gaze at the undefined, the unmediated, is hard to shake off; our newfound place of strangeness generates residues we carry around with us as strangeness and uncanniness press on us through reminders of the world's anxiety-inducing possibilities. So, anxiety is a profound awareness of myself as I am unmediated and naked, with no anchors to support my sense of self. When we enter the world, we find man has made man comprehensible, by covering up our being with layers of theory and knowledge and understanding and social construction; in our uncanny moments we notice we are naked underneath his manmade clothing. We are anxious because we do not know who we are and, indeed, are afraid to find out, for this is not a matter of discovery but of unguided invention and painful construction. (For Tillich too, our contingent existence made us anxious: the contingency of the fact that we exist in this time, in this place, in this way, with this perspective; all of this could have been some other way, and still could be. We were never necessary or required; we were placed here fortuitously and accidentally and will be ejected in due course.)

Our reckoning of our contingency is not just available for our identity; it is extensible to everything in this world. What is this thing we call a "hammer"? It has a name and a function, but it has a meaning and identity only within a constructed network of meanings; this is a "handle," this is a "head," each named and identified for us similarly; this is the "nail" it hammers into tables we make. Man-made objects are contingent; what about material and matter itself? Those are mere shadows too, modern physics informs us, ripples in a field that permeates all space, dependent for their identity on our measurements; if we learn enough metaphysics, we find even the basic elements of existence, our basic units of measurement and analysis, are named and identified by us; the "natural kinds" like "chemical elements" are placed there by our scientific theories and their conceptual schemes; the world that we know, it turns out, is man-made. As the American pragmatist philosopher William James noted, "the trail of the human serpent is thus over everything."[91] A trail that includes ours: anxiety informs us we have a chance to make a distinctive contribution to these traces.

When we experience the defamiliarization induced by such existential anxiety, we are profoundly shaken; we experience profound shifts in perspective that make us consider the world anew as beauty, and terror too, as heaven and hell. The disorientation or alarm and paranoia or cosmic terror on "bad trips" caused by psychotropic and psychedelic substances such as cannabis or LSD often results from their induction of this strangeness, this uncanny state; it is caused by this self-dissolution, this loss of self, of all that is known and familiar. As many a psychonaut caught up in the psychedelic maelstrom realizes, the most important task our parents accomplished with their loving care was to attune us to the strangeness of reality, the greatest trip of all. They prepared us for that push out the door into the strangeness outside, one tamed by the elaborate, yet contingent systems of human meaning imposed on it. The world's preoccupations, virtuous distractions that define "normal," keep us sane. But other arrangements, other networks of meanings, were possible; this revelation that this world is not the only one possible is a frightening prospect for those who consider its stability and invariance essential to their sanity.

When I am possessed by the mood of anxiety, I find myself outside the conventional world of accepted meanings; I have lost my constructed, earthly role-bound self and confront instead my nothingness, my lack of a self before I decide what self I might be. The self given to me by the world to occupy a public slot is a front I use to navigate its affairs; when that mask is removed, what lies beneath is formless and misshapen, awaiting definition by my choices. I cannot reduce myself to the notion of a conventional man, this mythical *Das Man*—complete with social roles and desirable end points for a life—that I was fervently reassured was my civilization's highest goal for me to attain. I feel alone; here I am disoriented, the outsider, alone in possessing a vision that renders the constructed world inauthentic, and its other residents deluded zombies whose own painful self-realization awaits.

I face, now, my own limitation, my own circumscribed and limited life, marked off by death on one side, and prebirth on the other. Once I am dead, I will be nothing. This realization, prompted by my experience of anxiety and its accompanying uncanny state, can cause me to act, to choose, or to cower in the corner. As I commit to this world, this life, even as my inevitable death stands over it, I must commit fully to my choices and actions at every instant of my life, for my existence depends on it. This realization *may* cause me to seize the world anew and confront my true being as being-in-the-world, responsible for making it. We have not just inherited the world; we have a role to play in it; our path forward is paved by our choices.

For Heidegger, it is a mistake to think of death as a biological phenomenon, a future event like any other, one that we can avoid thinking about, something that happens to others with the status of a remote abstract truth. But this "fleeing in the face of death,"[92] which relies on outright denial and dishonesty, is a fleeing in the face of ourselves. When we, in a state of strangeness, alone, with all our made-up relationships to the world terminated, are brought before the possibility of our death, we realize our mode of existence is that of an entity hurtling toward its own effacement, extinguishment, and eventual nothingness. We attain an acute understanding of death; when we take death on as a possibility that suffuses our life, we attain a momentous item of knowledge, as we realize that nonexistence, the counterpart of existence, is possible at every moment. When we accept our death, we are liberated, for we are open to what may happen at any instant, with no false comfort; our possibilities become provisional. We stand free of a pointless absorption in the constructed weekday world and understand our existence as limited, shaped, and formed by our mortality. As these brute constraints of existence are sharply defined, our life acquires clarity and definition in turn.

Anxiety then is an informant of who we are, of what kind of being we are, of the kind of self we can have if we choose to. Our *existential* conscience, rather than functioning as the hectoring moralizer of conventional ethics, urges us to confront and work through our anxiety, to assume responsibility for our lives, free of guilt and fear of disapproval. This existential conscience, the voice of anxiety, is heard as an alien voice in our everyday existence; it is a call to investigate our true nature, to listen, to notice who we are and what we can become. But we are so absorbed by the world's demands that we do not heed this call or try to suppress and repress it; or we may misunderstand it and medicate it. We may, as most people do, render the conscience an external societal or cultural phenomenon and adopt conventional, mainstream, everyday ethics.[93] But to envisage our conscience as objective and formalized, consisting of obligation to venerable religious beliefs, principles of reason, or societal mores, is to misunderstand the call of the *existential* conscience. In our authentic existence we must acknowledge our limitations, and recognize that in choosing one action, we irrevocably preclude others, that with each positive act, we murder infinitely many other existences.

This world's diversions, and our own "defense mechanisms," enable us to repress our awareness of those dreaded anxious moods that peek in on us uninvited. But existence does not permit these facile defenses to survive, allowing anxiety to repeatedly invade our inner citadels. We repair the damage but remain subject to intrusions and reminders, which make the world precarious, and which generate the uncanny instead. This experience of "not-being-at-home-in-the-world" is suffused with an awareness of death, now understood as the "impossibility of further possibility," and the contingent nature of our existence.[94] We live thus in a state of utter possibility, threatened all the while by the certain destruction of all possibilities. We are creatures aware of utter uncertainty and certainty; one acts as a creator of terrifying eventuality, the other of a final, terrifying unknowing. We are the being aware that now is not all there is, that there lurks a past behind and a future ahead. We have regretful memory and fearful anticipation; we are set to be anxious in inquiring, acting, choosing, and living in incompleteness and uncertainty. Indeed, the acute trifecta of existential parameters, that we are in time, that this time is finite, and that we are aware of that fact, ensures that we will always be anxious; the possession of memory and anticipation ensures we will ascribe to ourselves an enduring self and personhood, but it also means we resign ourselves to anxiety over its fates and fortunes—as the Buddha noted.

Great works of existentialist literature often refer to characters who are isolated, made strange, and spiritually sick, like those of Albert Camus's classic *Stranger* or Richard Wright's *The*

Outsider; these central protagonists confront this world's utter absurdity again and again and find that their only solution, the only way to inject meaning into an existence that is meaningless, is by choice and decision and action. And a willingness to face up to the consequences of their choices: there is no signal the world will send our way to confirm our actions are the right ones, merely the hopeful assent of confused and uncertain humans like us.

In my life, my parents had ordered the world for me, made it comprehensible, made a place for me, told me it was mine. When they were gone, those reassurances and guarantees and place keepings were gone; when I became an orphan, the world became strange, and I lost my place within it, there to wander lonely and unwanted, cast adrift through a cruel and unforgiving landscape. But more than anything else, it was strange; I did not feel like I belonged. To find out "where" and "who" I was, I had to confront and work through the notion of an identity that had lost its intended moorings in home and family and nation; it is not a task that I anticipate will ever be complete, for any identity gained will always be provisional. Heidegger reminds us of the strangeness that is our persistent companion, a cruel and terrible presence that must be stared at in the face if we are to ever come to grips with who and what we are and might yet be.

The existentialists are united by an insistence on the freedom of man, and on the notion that anxiety is our indicator that we are constituted by a conscious awareness of it. They are not united by faith, nor by their notions of death and nothingness; but they do agree that confronting and working through anxiety is essential to our self-development. Indeed, it is in these confrontations that our self-development arises; we are those creatures whose becoming is crucially dependent on our encounters with, and resolutions of, anxiety. Anxiety was a crucial signifier too, in another intellectual domain, that of psychoanalysis, a discipline that owes its foundations to philosophers like Arthur Schopenhauer, Nietzsche, and Kierkegaard, and which understood anxiety as a pointer to internal conflict, one that needed to be resolved if personal growth were to continue. Without that resolution, neuroticisms, phobias, and disorders resulted.

REPRESSION, CONFLICT, MEMORABLE TRAUMA

For Sigmund Freud, anxiety was central to psychoanalysis; it was an elusive emotion and concept he defined and redefined more than once to place it into its appropriate location in the human psyche; his struggles to encapsulate its diverse relationships with the panoply of disorders, phobias, and neuroses it appeared to underwrite shows he was—often ruefully—aware of its complexity and manifold natures.[1] Anxiety could be understood, simultaneously, as an ontological feature of human existence—if you were born, you were anxious—and as a contingent feature of our biological, psychological, and cultural responses to this world and the civilizations we had erected to master it, for anxiety (thanks to its persistent companion, guilt) was a response to its imposed strictures and demanding morals and standards. It arose, too, from the structure of the human mind, for Freud's notion of anxiety crucially depended on the psychoanalytic theoretical apparatus: the libido; the libidinal object; the unconscious; drives, frustrated or otherwise; the id, the ego, the superego, and the complex interactions between them. Anxiety could be understood as a signal of conflict in the relational dynamics of the mind described by such an abstract theoretical model. Importantly, anxiety was dependent on individual psychology interacting with the social environment; each notion of anxiety that Freud developed was in some way a result of an idiosyncratic interaction with, or an internal conflict related to, the world "outside."

Stripped to its fundamentals, in the culminating psychoanalytic view, anxiety is our fearful response to a world destined to not satisfy our deepest needs; its analysis reflects a tragic view of existence. This world will cause us painful, terrifying losses again and again; anxiety marks the trajectory of our lives as we move from one real loss to other imagined losses, remembering past traumas and activating older fears as we do so. Anxiety appears as a source of *self-knowledge* because it is through our experience of it that we detect the presence of inner conflict in our psyche and realize we live in a divided, not unitary, house; that we understand that within us lurks repression—in response to this world's guilt-inducing restrictions; that we realize we have suffered losses in our history whose recurrence we fear in our lives; and that we live our lives threatened by, and fearfully anticipating, a familiar yet archaic loss. Our ability to *not expect* an imagined, painfully remembered security the world cannot ever again provide for us is the key to integrating our anxieties into our evolving selves.

Within the psychoanalytic framework, anxiety was the basis of all psychopathologies, a fundamental crisis in the mind that underwrote others: the more severe the anxiety, the more severe the associated mental illness, and the greater the task of the psychoanalyst (and analysand). Resolving anxiety by easing the repression exercised by the mind, resolving inner conflict, reconciling oneself to earlier losses and moving on without a beloved "lost object," became central to resolving the associated mental illness. To move on and through life, confronting anxiety as we did so, was a sign of emotional and psychological maturity for Freud, just as it was for Kierkegaard; both held that a fundamental inner conflict or "blockage" had to be eased by a process of "working through." If for Kierkegaard and the existentialists failures to resolve anxiety resolved in an unmade self, then for Freud and psychoanalysis failure to resolve anxiety left us with a scarred and conflict-ridden self—a neurotic one—living in, and haunted by, the past. Our anxiety was a signal ghosts were our mental companions; we jumped in response to imagined shadows and terrors, investing mundane events with an overstated significance just because they reminded us of our actual past losses and fears. We were not living in the present; we were living in the past, children of a kind, living a perpetual infancy.

Resolving anxiety through psychoanalysis, then, required us to become adults, to accept that a loss had occurred in the past, and that others inevitably would too. If we did not acknowledge the first loss, and our fearful reaction to it, we were destined to repeat that trauma. To work through our anxiety was to understand ourselves through an analytical archaeology and genealogy that led to self-knowledge and self-reconciliation and acceptance. The notion of "reconciliation" is especially important; psychoanalysis urged us to move on without the comforting illusions of childhood and the hopes they had engendered in a being destined to move on alone that it would always have companionship, care, and security. We were alone, utterly alone, and psychoanalysis urged us to accept this fact and face up to its consequences. Rather than asking us to wallow in primitive childhood affect, it urged an adult response—to acknowledge that parental love and care was a unique occurrence, one not to be repeated in our lives. Psychoanalysis required a radical acceptance of this world as is: we could not avoid birth, for it was in the past; we could not avoid the literal or figurative loss of the mother—no matter what form that maternal care took in our lives; we could not avoid living alone, for even when we thought we had found partners and loves, they would never give us the companionship and care we enjoyed as children. Deny these incontrovertible constraints of reality, through defense mechanisms, through the production of anxiety, and you invited neurosis. Anxiety was that crucial signal that indicated we were conflict ridden and repressed—and needed psychoanalysis.

For Freud, there were three theoretical developments of anxiety over time. Anxiety was understood first via the so-called toxic theory of the libido; then as causing internal, self-directed repression, and finally, as a signal of impending danger, which warned the self or, the ego, that an impending, familiar-because-remembered situation of abandonment and helplessness was about to ensue. Freud's first formulation of anxiety treated it as a biological phenomenon; the second as a signal of unconscious inner psychic conflict between the untrammeled desires of the uninhibited id, the realistic ego, and the morally repressive superego; the third treated the mind as a theater for the recollection of loss, as anxiety becomes a signal of traumatic events, a way to anticipate and prepare for trauma. As Freud came to believe, "the Ego was the seat of anxiety,"[2] for it was its tempestuous, conflict-ridden relationship to the id and the superego that was crucially productive and determinant of anxiety.

Freud's first, "toxic theory" of anxiety suggested it was a *transformation* of libido caused by physiological failure or external repression; here, anxiety was unreleased, dammed up libidinal energy, reflecting tension and frustration, created by the failure to properly satisfy our libido's demands.[3] In this formulation, Freud understood anxiety to result from a failure to discharge an essential tension that must find release. Sexual inability was one such critical failure to discharge libido, to find relief; its paradigmatic sufferers were the incompetent, nervous, fumbling bridegroom on a wedding night; the righteous saint practicing abstinence within the confines of a repressive institution; the Catholic husband forced to use the rhythm method for birth control: in each case, sexual energy was not discharged and was transformed into a toxic brew, anxiety. It is not anxiety about sexual performance that causes the bridegroom to not be able to perform; rather, it is the physiological failure of the sexual performance that causes anxiety; it is not anxiety that prevents the saint from indulging in sex, but rather the external code of chastity required by his vows; anxiety resulted from his failure to find sexual release. Anxiety, then, resulted from, or was caused by, external repression.

In Freud's second theory too, there is repression, for when the ego fails to manage, redirect, or satisfy the id's morally forbidden or dangerous desires or emotions, anxiety causes the desires of the id to be repressed by the ego. The crucial difference here is that the repression is internal, caused by one part of the mind against another, by the anxious reaction of one mental component to the expressed desires of another. This anxiety is a signature of conflict in our mind, its reaction to the social world, to its associated realistic constraints and moral demands. For the price of our civilized world, our departure from nature, is a repression occasioned by anxiety; our world's sexual morality, the basis of familial structure and social groupings, relies on guilt-ridden frustration, internal and external, of those of our desiring drives found intolerable by it.[4] Anxiety is a signal to us that we harbor repressed emotions, desires, and sexuality; the task of psychoanalysis—and the analyst and analysand—was to allow an investigation of such repression to aid a working through of the anxiety and an easing of the repression. Crucially, this does not mean that we express the repressed desire and act on it; rather, it means we acknowledge the existence of this desire and think through what it means for our relationship to the object in question, and to our lived present. Neither of these steps is trivial; hence the all-too-common intractability of the psychoanalytic process.[5]

The first formulation of anxiety considered it externally repressed, and thereby transformed, libido; the second formulation considered it evidence of internal conflict as the ego and the superego repressed the id, not allowing it to express morally dangerous desires (the harboring of which occasioned guilt in us). Here, anxiety created internal forces of repression as opposed to the external forces of conformance creating anxiety in the first model. The psychoanalytic focus on anxiety goes from social to individual: the world does not repress and police me; I, my own mind, do. Anxiety thus produced repression, and not the other way around; Freud termed "neurotic anxiety" as such because it causes neurosis, not because it is caused by neurosis. In this model of anxiety arising from inner conflict, to have a desire but also to believe that that desire is immoral or dangerous is to suffer guilt and anxiety; we approach the forbidden fruit, and yet we shrink from it; we are made anxious. This should remind us of Kierkegaard!

For Freud, the anxiety that caused repression—when the morally censorious superego attacked the ego or the prudent ego resisted the id's desiring demands—engendered "defense mechanisms" and in turn, the neurotic symptoms of phobias and disorders. The internal, threatening, instinctual demand—like incestuous sexual desire for a family member or anger at a parent, friend, or lover who could withdraw their affection—was the root of neurotic anxiety. We are afraid of our desires or our expressions of problematic emotions, like anger, and fight to suppress them, to restrict them, to keep them hidden—not just from the world outside, but from ourselves too. (Sometimes these repressed desires find expression in mysterious, surreal dreams.) But once we displace that fear onto some element of the world, we have a visible phobia or disorder. An agoraphobic, someone scared of open spaces, is made anxious by their forbidden desires—perhaps the sexual desire of a lustful son for his mother—and has displaced it onto an open space. This fear, made visible, external, and concrete can be mastered; open spaces can be avoided, whereas the forbidden desire springs on us uninvited and uncontrollable, evidence that we ourselves are out of control. Neuroses, then, offered a substitute form of satisfaction of repressed desires, preferable to repressing the impulse, for if the impulse was denied, anxiety ensued.[6] *The avoidance of a particular kind of anxiety* is the patient's "gain" from the symptom and its associated and resultant neurosis. (This suggestion, that supposedly irrational emotions are experienced and understood as rational within an internal schema for the sufferer, is a signal theoretical innovation on Freud's part.)

Freud's notion of sexual repression causing anxiety is illuminating considering the social policing and regulation of sex in late nineteenth-century Vienna and other European venues, but what of cultures and civilizations like ours, which by their advertised, public demands for sexual performance and success breed an anxiety over sexual inadequacy, an anxiety about sexual failure? For we face in our society the problem of punishment not for performance but for *nonperformance* instead: our cultures saturate us with images of idealized potential romantic partners and sexual performers with perfect bodies; online, and elsewhere, we are fed a daily dose of sexual inadequacy, insecurity, and frustration. We are not sexual enough; we are not beautiful or sexually active enough; our list of "conquests" seems pitifully small; women, of course, have been, and still are, censured, persecuted, and policed for their sexuality. Given that we spend so much time on our bodies dieting, working out, and posing for Instagram photos, should we not be having more sex, better sex, more gymnastic and spectacular sex—the way other people on social media seem to be? The modern phenomenon of "incels" is underwritten by both misogyny and an acute anxiety over sexual failure in a world that glories in public displays of sexuality and sexual success. The incel finds an expression for their anxiety over sexual failure in their misogyny: Why am I to be denied sex when so many lucky people have all the sex they want? Why do women deny me sexual access when they are not bound by social restriction? They must be dispensing their sexual favors elsewhere; why not to me?

In such a society, one saturated with images and representations of desire and sex, monogamy appears a particularly perverse social arrangement—especially given the amount of time we are supposed to be spending on our bodies buffing ourselves for unavailable sexual pleasures. The cultural role sexual performance and insecurity and jealousy play is significantly determinative of our sense of sexual inadequacy: we can be made anxious not just by sexual failure and sexual underperformance, but, in our culture, by our failure to live up to the sexual ideals relentlessly flogged by our cultures. We did not have sex with enough people, with the right people; for women, this sexual anxiety navigates the patriarchal burden of needing to be sexual and chaste alike, a recipe for cognitive dissonance. Pornography—which saturates our online spaces—makes our sexuality inadequate; our personal sex lives seem pallid and insipid in comparison. We might have all the sex we want and yet remain sexually dissatisfied, a new understanding of sexual failure. Our modern environment may be an anxiety-inducing one for reasons the converse of those Freud imagined.

In Freud's matured and final theory of anxiety, a deep and primeval anxiety was occasioned by birth, the most traumatic, dramatic event of all, our sundering from the safest of refuges. Birth is the template and prototype of later trauma, its shadow falling over subsequent anxieties experienced by the individual, whose mind replayed an earlier event "to cope with an identical event should it occur in the future." This kind of anxiety was a *signaling mental state,* one in which a "reenactment of a past event" allowed reminiscing about the past and forecasting the future.[7] Anxiety is a signal we that remember the past; we sense and anticipate the repetition of a situation for which there lurks a primitive reaction in the psyche: the utter helplessness we felt as a child. This was a state peculiar to humans, for no other offspring was quite as helpless in its unfamiliar environment outside the womb as the human.

Freud distinguished between an anxiety that was a primitive reaction to a traumatic situation—like birth, or the loss of maternal love—that occurred early in life, and an anxiety that invoked that earlier primitive anxiety all over again. In the case of the former, "reaction anxiety," the still-developing child feels overwhelmed because of real or perceived danger; this danger is averted because the child expects help to counter the threat, and indeed in our childhood, such assistance is usually available thanks to our comforting parents, who magically appear out of the mist to lend a helping hand. *Anxiety is the resurrected fear of the loss of an object whose presence once offered protection against a dangerous situation in which we were helpless.* Different life stages—as befitting their psychoanalytic status as distinct developmental stages—produced different fears and associated different objects with them as saviors. When we were separated from mother, we resurrected the trauma of birth; when we suffered the wrath of the superego and feared losing its love and care, we resurrected the fear of the loss of the mother. The anxiety about social condemnation or the loss of social status due to the conflict between the ego and the superego and the id was as acute as it was because it resurrected primal fears of the loss of the mother object, or depending on the developmental stage, the fear of castration.

There were two distinct stages in the creation of neurotic anxiety. First, an anxiety overwhelmed us at a traumatic situation in life and then later, a secondary anxiety anticipated a recurrence of that situation, triggering the various defense mechanisms of neuroses, phobias, and disorders, now understood as symptoms of an unresolved anxiety. The primal traumatic states were experienced as we were born and invoked at later stages in life when crucial losses—the loss of a libidinal object, the loss of the libidinal object's love—occurred. Freud was fond of saying "the finding of an object is in fact a refinding of it,"[8] that when we found romantic partners or job satisfaction we were recreating an older pleasure, an older attachment of the libido to an external object; in the same fashion, "every loss was a repetition," for the mind was a theater in which primal traumas were restaged in different guises, springing out at us from life's corners, triggering in us again and again that primary, terrifying encounter with birth and evoking the possibility of the loss of the favored object we once held dear.

Distinct forms of anxiety, then, haunt each stage of psychic life, just because the losses we suffer at each stage are distinctive: the loss of the womb; the loss of the breast and the mother in our infancy; the diminution of parental love and caring as we become individualized; these are re-created and staged by the mind as we make our way through the world. In a crucial resonance with Tillich's notion of mundane losses being reminders of our eventual nothingness, we are bound to experience anxiety as we move through life just because it is all too easy for us to assimilate the mundane, daily, trivial loss to the cosmic, primal traumas of birth, of the separation from the "good mother."

So, in Freud's mature theory of anxiety, our psychic life is shaped by the primordial experience of birth anxiety, which serves as a template for later forms of anxious experience. It is birth, separation, and castration, not death, that are the primeval anxieties; our anxiety feels like a fear of "no-thing" because it is an obscured fear of a historical event; a concrete fear, for instance, the fear of the loss of the mother, has been covered with layers of time; the traumatic event is not remembered directly but only through its anxious traces in our unconscious. That lurking presence is why anxiety feels like a shadowy, nonlocatable unease. Our episodes of anxiety recall these shadowy dangers, especially that of the trauma of birth; indeed, as Freud would insist, every anxiety we experience is in some way a reinvocation of this most traumatic of life events. The "real" trauma responsible for anxiety occurred early in life; later anxiety functioned as a signal of anticipated danger once the memory of the traumatic event—a terrifying, memorable one—was repressed and its attendant affect transformed to anxiety. Freud emphasized the affect of "helplessness," for anxiety was our primal reaction to that feeling, so characteristic of the human infant, one that we would reproduce later in life as a call for help in the face of anticipated trauma.

A few choice quotes from Freud help us think about his conceptions of anxiety in his final formulations. First, our primary anxiety is "the loss of the object [of maternal care]."[9] This spoke to the concrete fear of a loss of the mother, the fear of "feeling the loss of the loved (longed for) person."[10] And of course, if there was some emotion that we expressed that made us lose the love of a loved one, then our mind would be anxious about expressing that emotion ever again for fear of losing someone or something, a loss that would remind us of the first terrible loss we had suffered. For the rest of our lives, "loss of love ... becomes a new and far more enduring danger and occasion for anxiety."[11] For each loss of love is a reminder of the primal loss of a very privileged "object," the mother, that followed our birth, which is now understood as the fount of our primeval anxiety. Every real or imagined loss, then, the disapproval of a family member or of a friend dropping us from their "in-list," the anger of a supervisor at work threatening unemployment, the mysterious coldness of a good friend—becomes a shadow of the primeval loss; this world, in consonance with Freud's tragic view of existence, does not and will not satisfy our desire for a love like the maternal.

The quantity and quality of a parent's affection toward their children, then, may have a potent effect on the level of anxiety those children will experience later in life. Anxiety in adults may be a function of early childhood abandonment—in whatever form—by parents; the more parents withhold affection or are selective in granting it, the more anxious the child may be; parental bereavement, of course, would then be the worst form of anxiety-inducing abandonment (as it had seemed to be in my case). If your parents give you a secure environment, one in which you do not fear or suffer the loss of their parental love in capricious or cruel ways, you might be protected against this form of anxiety; if not, you may not be. An anxious parent can be less loving and attentive just because they are so wrapped up in their anxieties; the anxious signals they give off can make their kids anxious too. Early losses and deprivations of affection and care in our life, then, may instill deep-rooted fears about the recurrence of such losses—no matter what their new form. Our friend who does not return our call causes as much anxiety as she does because the meaning we attach to this failure of friendship is not trivial; it is a reminder of a terrible loss we had once suffered and might yet suffer again.

So, after traveling through his various formulations, Freud's matured and final view of anxiety was that its roots lay in the most primal of human events, our birth, and was triggered or reactivated, by mundane events in our lives. Because the trauma of birth is foretold, as are later losses, we are destined to experience anxiety; it is the dreadful signature of our lives. If every "finding," every "discovery" of person or object, was a "re-finding," a "rediscovery" of a lost object, then every loss, real or threatened, was a loss all over again of a significant lost libidinal object. Because each developmental stage was marked by and characterized by a peculiar and distinctive loss whose recurrence we feared and because the world was destined to cause us losses, we would live our lives anxiously, disproportionately anticipating and responding to empirical fears because we were haunted by the past.

Freud's analysis of "separation anxiety" made obvious sense to me; I had lost my parents; they were gone at the fair, never to return; if that solidity could be taken away, nothing could be reassuring. I was destined to find the world especially fearful, because every loss—even as trivial as missing a train, failing an exam, or suffering the withdrawal of the affections of a girlfriend—was a reminder of a shattering, terrifying loss. I did not see and understand and interpret this world's losses like others did; my idiosyncratic history made it the case that the meaning I assigned to my losses was far darker. I now understood why I always frantically returned my friends' calls, accepted their every invitation, even as I resented their selective acceptances of mine; I was too scared to lose the comforts and companionship they represented, too scared of the loss of their love. My jealousy was a profound indicator of my anxiety; any potential loss of the love I thought I enjoyed was occasion for nauseating anxiety and paralyzing anger. My background as an immigrant could not be understated; I had suffered the loss of a great deal that was familiar and comforting—indeed, an entire life—when I left home. Other losses would always be a reminder of those traumatic separations, of all that I had lost in the bargain.

Freud's theoretical formulations, and the accompanying speculative interpretation of the phenomenology of our anxious experiences, ask us to reconsider our psychological orientation to our stations in the social and material world that surrounds us: How worried are we about the condemnation of culture, society, and friends of the life we live, the choices we make? How well have we accepted, and reconciled ourselves to, the permanent loss of parental security and care? How secure do we feel in our personal and professional relationships? Do we persistently demand parental care and love from our friends and lovers, an examination they are destined to fail? The relationship between anxiety and guilt in Kierkegaard finds an acute resonance here: Are we anxious, or are we guilty? What is the difference for us? What demand or constraint are we (supposedly) guilty of not satisfying or adhering to?

The emphasis of Freudian psychoanalysis on inner psychic conflict, its acknowledgment of the role that civilizations and cultures play in repressing our instincts, and the importance of (often policed and repressed) sexuality in its relationship to neuroses crucially illuminates our anxiety. Freud's analysis is useful, for instance, in helping us understand a species of anxiety termed "social anxiety"; people are fearful of the disapproval of others, of losing friends and family if they express their needs or speak up about their hurt or alienation in a relationship; the fear we feel as we approach the precipice of a personal conflict is a reminder that we fear the termination of the relationship whose terms we are merely attempting to negotiate. The gay man who fears coming out fears not just familial and social disapproval but the loss of his friends and family; the anticipation of this loss can be acutely anxiety provoking especially if it is an echo of an earlier event we found traumatic. The same applies to the loss of a job, a friendship, a lover, even a workmate whose disapproval becomes a stand-in for the disapproval of the superego.

Finally, consider that antidepressants are often said to produce the lessening of sexual desire (a "damping" of the libido in psychoanalytic terms); such a neutered person is, of course, free of the anxiety of sexual performance, of the social anxiety of needing to impress others sexually, or of losing sexual partners. Do antidepressants work then because they make us feel less anxious (and depressed) about sexual failure or of a failure to meet my culture's sexual standards? Does such a dampened libido decrease our exposure to the anxiety over "sexual losses" in personal relationships?

Freud's emphasis on the relationship between our forms of life, our constructed civilization, and our social world brings us to the alienating and dehumanizing encounters between self and society as the ground for anxiety. The existentialists saw the social as a refuge for inauthenticity, and anxiety as the hallmark of our freedom. The critical materialist tradition considers the social to be the creator of our anxiety as it denied us our freedom: our feeling of anxiety was not the feeling of freedom; it was the feeling of living life in a world constructed on someone else's terms, something that had turned my individuality, my chosen life, into merely a means for their ends. (In case you were wondering, yes, there are important resonances between the critical materialist tradition and Nietzsche's formulations.) The anxiety we felt was that of a profoundly alienated creature, living in a strange land, not the master of its destiny, not the architect of its fate, controlled, quantified, and pushed hither and thither by man-made forces. To cure anxiety was to do no less than to choose to live in a world constructed differently, a task for social and political critique and activism. Mere theory would not help us understand or ameliorate our anxiety; praxis was required too.

ANXIETY AND THE SOCIAL

We have always suspected that this world's arrangements and the behavior of other humans make us anxious, for human history and its circumstances inform and shape human consciousness (and vice versa, in a codetermining relationship). Our fundamental existential or psychoanalytic anxiety must then find tangible expression and manifestation through the material circumstances and cultural arrangements of our lives; the resultant anxieties that afflict us will vary by the cultural forms we are embedded in, by the socioeconomic histories that precede us. In the United States, the land of the free and home of the brave, the most medicated, most economically unequal nation in the world, financial fears and anxieties run rampant; elsewhere, other fears—political (war), social (civil unrest, legal persecutions of minorities), and geographic (climate change)—stalk the land. The anxiety of the eighteenth-century European differed from that of the twentieth-century Asian or the nineteenth-century American, located as it was in a novel cultural and psychical space. If our social, political, and economic moral circumstances are different in the twenty-first, we should expect to find we are anxious in our own distinctive way. Every era, every age, every epoch produces its own distinctive fears and cultural anxieties, transmitted by parents, friends, teachers;

by the music that plays in parties and cars, the messages on the advertisements and billboards; in the snatches of conversations the child hears through partially open doors.

Each culture and time produce too its own form of death and nothingness, its distinctive style of writing us out of our imagined home within it to alienate us, to exacerbate our existential isolation; modern man's most distinctive signature is a forlorn eviction from his former homes, moral and spiritual. The "death of God" was an alienation from spiritual solace and comfort, an anxiety-causing encounter with Godlessness and the loss of a cosmic telos and moral order; the Copernican heliocentric model was a sundering from an imagined heavenly mooring, an alienation from safer, more consoling cosmologies; the Freudian revolution was a profound making strange of oneself, a division of ourselves into the known and unknown. Following or accompanying these historically valorized revolutions, the many cultural, social, and scientific-technical revolutions of modernity brought with them uncertainties distinctive of those eras, leading to fervent and sincere proclamations of successive ages of anxiety. The radical transformations of the Industrial Revolution and the acute inequalities of the modern age (exacerbated by a rapacious colonialism and imperialism) spectacularly increased anxiety in those societies most profoundly affected by them; and as civilization marches on, leaving the debris of older social and cultural forms and now, thanks to climate change, our constructed world behind, anxiety seems to be increasing in strictly monotonic fashion. An acute symptom of this increased suffering in our contemporary world is that natal debates are increasing as we question whether we should even procreate, that is, fulfill our primal biological function, in a world with such an uncertain future. This is an acute moral question, one not faced in its contemporary dimensions by those who came before us, for they did not live in a world structured like ours, did not suffer our anxieties.

In the new millennium, too, we have been informed of the "male anxiety" of those confronted in the workplace and at home by the presence of women empowered by feminist ideals; the "white anxiety" of those confronted with a racially enlightened world and its demands for social justice and tangible and intangible reparations; the "economic anxiety" underwriting a lurch toward populist and authoritarian regimes in the West and the East. These anxieties build on the uncertainties we and our fellow citizens experience about our social standing and prospects (our status) in the face of the complexity of our economic and financial systems, and the rapid, unsettling political and technological change they induce and sustain. These modern anxieties are underwritten by fears of displacement, of effacement, of a spiritual and moral death that wipes out older, established, reassuring forms of life and power relations, only to replace them with those unknown and unspecified, a glaring nothingness at the heart of the visible future. The archetypal immigrant displaced from an older home and subjected to the bewildering changes of the new world, the loss of families and friends, suffers high rates of anxiety, depression, and alcoholism; that is precisely our lot, for at one profound level, we are all immigrants, displaced, lost, and disoriented even in climes previously considered familiar. We have lost our older homes and struggle to find our way around this one.

This perfunctory nod to the historical and material circumstances of anxiety suggests, as it did to an existentialist theologian like Tillich, that anxiety is evoked and blossoms when the "normal" fails; it resonates too with the Freudian notion that a primeval anxiety reoccurs when the safety of the protective parental structure is lost. As Tillich suggested, it is when "accustomed structures of meaning, power, belief, and order disintegrate" that our existential anxiety finds new garbs and manifestations, as the resultant new material conditions conspire to amplify anxiety realized and experienced in a highly specific form.[1] Tillich offers us the acute example of Depression-era America, a "highly competitive society" whose individuals experienced the "loss of an economic basis."[2] The damage of those terrible times was not merely financial; the mental toll it exerted was just as significant as families and social groupings alike crumbled, subjected to the unbearable stresses of the loss of employment, dignity, and the means to keep body and soul together in the face of an advancing eventual personal extinction. (This commentary should be familiar to those who lived through the Covid-19 pandemic of 2020–22.)

A questioning and reconfiguration of the "normal" is, of course, our new normal; we are confronted by a bewildering array of normative standards,[3] by social and political systems fluid in status and established norms; we do not now have our stations in life assigned to us, rather we freely choose them, an anxiety-causing burden familiar to the existentialist. Our endless and continuing stratification of society—along with its desirable possibilities of "upward mobility"—engenders perennial agonizing over our social and moral adequacy as we move between communities with diverse values and notions of meaningfulness; we cannot stop engaging in relentless, invidious comparison ("the thief of joy"),[4] and obsessively worry about the loss of status were we to lose our economic standing.

From these vantage points, anxiety will not seem like an encounter with authenticity or freedom; it will feel like a punishment, a wallowing in misery. Indeed, here, anxiety will seem like an acute form of unfreedom, of the loss of possibility, of the ever presence of restriction, constraint, and forcible passage along predetermined avenues. Such considerations could make us question, in its entirety, the valorization of anxiety as a hallmark of freedom by the existentialists; after all, does not such an anxiety make us feel less free, more constrained? That is, the more anxious I feel, am I the less free, just because my anxiety constrains me and makes it impossible for me to act? When I am anxious, do I not see less, experience less, in the restricted world that I now occupy? Anxious people are fearful and cautious, the very antithesis of freedom. An anxious person suffers by making their world smaller, not larger by the invocation of the possibilities that Kierkegaard valorizes. And of course, given that many anxious persons fear losing control, does such freedom of unrestricted choice and action seem desirable? Such a piercing anxiety can make us "escape from freedom" into the arms of—pick your authoritarian poison—Nazis, totalitarian communism, fascism, faux democracies beholden to economic overlords, anything to provide security from the gnawing, nail-biting, nauseating anxiety resultant from an encounter with the novel and uncertain.[5] These responses show that while the existentialist understanding of anxiety is that it is a signature of our freedom, it is not always experienced as such. But it also helps us understand why we, as anxious people, seek to exert control over our lives, as we strive to keep our freedom at bay: we frenetically regulate ourselves, our diets, our actions, our moods, our social spaces and commitments.

Considerations of history, materiality, and culture in understanding anxiety provoke many questions: If anxiety is a basic human affect and signature of human consciousness, then why does it emerge only as an explicitly named and identified problem in the nineteenth century, as opposed to remaining an implicit signature in philosophical speculation earlier? Why have "mental illness" and its many "anxiety disorders" increased in the twentieth century? Do we diagnose more efficiently, or do we diagnose more so that we can medicate more—using medications manufactured for profit by large pharmaceutical companies? Was it the case that before we named and shamed anxiety, we were calling it some other mood or emotion, as the culture of the time required? Is there materiality in our times that makes anxiety into a problem it was not before? Has our culture found its own nomenclature for anxiety, naming new afflictions, providing new guises for a familiar foe?

Talk of anxiety in modern contexts cannot overlook our class, status, and economic insecurity; the indistinct fear of falling into the unplumbed abysses of unemployment, lowered income, and eventual penury is characteristic of modern middle-class anxiety. A singular modern achievement has been to replace the Great Chain of Being with the Great Hierarchy of Social and Economic Class and Status; we know what would await us were we to transgress in our socially and culturally defined and demanded responsibilities of relentless work, never-ending material accumulation, and undying ambition for class mobility. Class decline is our new death, the primeval sink of modern anxiety. If earlier traumas can lay down templates for future recurrences of anxiety, then consider a child being told relentlessly by their parents (and the world "outside") that they must "make something" of themselves, get a "good education" in the "right" venue, and a "good job"—or else! The pressure placed on the child to get these formative decisions correct is tremendous—for otherwise, our culture's distinctive death awaits. Our children, for their part, watch a persistent repeating show of their parents being anxious about their economic misfortunes; their anxious, overworked, financially stressed parents, produced by societies like ours, cannot fail to produce anxious children. Social observation can induce anxiety; quite simply, watching people get scared can make us scared; if we have grown up with anxious and scared parents, we are destined to be similarly afflicted. We live too, now, in a hyperconnected world, one in which all can be seen, heard, and posted, in which we are more self-conscious, and not always in a good way. We are more heavily surveilled, our futures controlled by impersonal, impenetrable combinations of man and machine, even as we sense that the world we have tamed can bite back any day—as the great Covid-19 pandemic of 2020–22 so painfully showed.

By the time we have grown up, we have watched our guardians shrink, cowering and terrified by this world's material forces; we have received warnings we may join them; and we wonder what this world's raison d'être is if its culturally recommended solutions produce economic inequality, climate change, and rampant mental illness. If the grand prizes of our civilization amount to long commutes, deprivation of time with family and friends, confinement in climate-controlled spaces while wearing uncomfortable clothes, bossy bosses who can hire and fire at will, and impossible-to-use vacation time, then why not reject it all? If not overtly, then perhaps inwardly, with a drooped shoulder, a dejected soul, an anxious heart? Perhaps we could just sink back into our couches at the end of an exhausting day devoted to building and sustaining someone else's fortunes and power, and light up, drink up, shoot up?

Our supposed agents of salvation, science and technology, have been of little help in ameliorating our anxieties, for modern technological changes disrupt older forms of social and political organization without dispelling older power forms or inequality and instead hurtle us toward climate change, mysterious pandemics, and political dysfunction. The twentieth and twenty first centuries have brought us a rude dispelling of the scientific dream into a nightmare: our greatest advances make the verdant earth uninhabitable while we remain paralyzed by our technical comforts, unwilling and unable to let go of the poisons that are killing us. As for medicine, even as it promises to deliver us from the terrifying afflictions of old, we often find its solutions too expensive for most of us. The great coronavirus pandemic of 2020–22 was a reminder that civilizational forces had not made the world safer; instead, we had unleashed deadlier forces on ourselves. The Covid-19 vaccines produced in record time were a scientific deliverance, a triumph of modern medicine and its technological apparatus, but the disaster of the pandemic was man-made. The political dysfunction visible in the United States in its public health responses to the pandemic were a reminder that we may master nature, but the mastery of human nature remains a perpetual challenge.

The resultant crisis of cynicism about modern technologies and indeed science itself, our supposed deliverance, creates a new age of anxiety. Such fears of our technical advancement are not new, as anyone who lived through the Cold War and partook of the feverish cultural products of that time can tell you; they have just found distinctive expression in this era. We have become aware of even greater monsters that lurk in our midst, sometimes human ones, and of their capacity to harness natural and technical forces to unleash destruction; we have been made aware that we are ever more cogs in a vast industrial and financial machine owned and controlled by a faceless and nameless few, that our children are growing up in a world destined for perdition if we do not change our ways.

Some variations of these fears have always lurked in the human psyche even as their newer forms find expression in our bodies and minds. We talk more about anxiety now; we exchange notes on our anxious experiences; we are more self-conscious about our anxiety. We have named many of our older fears and watched yet other novel ones come to be. Along with the promise of our financialized and technologized culture to turn us into *Das Man* is also the promise to turn us into the nothingness of our society: the homeless, the mentally ill, the incarcerated, the socially marginalized and condemned. We have been forced to look on this "refuse" ever since the day we were born, forced to investigate the fates that await if we insist on nonconformance with our society's orderings and demands. Our great foretold disasters are laid out on our sidewalks: the homeless, the sick, the indigent, the abandoned; our prisons are filled with those who transgressed socially. We know that if they had made enough money, been born into the right families or race, they would have saved themselves from this fate. Our societies, by insisting on an atomized social ordering, a casting to the fates in the name of individual freedom, all the while constructing social and economic structures that constrain our actual exercise of that liberty, threaten to turn us over to the "nasty, brutish, and short" life.[6] Our greatest fear is economic immiseration, for we know from that eventuality flow all disasters of our times: the destitution of our children, an untreatable illness, early death. That is our greatest fear: our greatest anxiety. During the Covid-19 pandemic, as I wrote this book, that anxiety became concretized into tangible fear. We did not feel free then; we felt oppressed, hounded, marginalized. How is the anxious person of our times to be told that the anxiety they feel is the hallmark of authentic moral and metaphysical freedom? Should they be so told?

An acerbic critical theorist and the original radical professor of philosophy, a prominent member of the Frankfurt school of critical theory, Herbert Marcuse was severely critical of existentialism, in particular, Sartre's *Being and Nothingness*, for claiming that the anxiety and meaninglessness that were distinctive features of the modern capitalist world and its stratified societies were the very nature of existence. Marcuse suggested thus that existentialism "hypothesizes specific historical conditions of human existence into ontological and metaphysical characteristics."[7] That is, existentialism takes contingent features of human existence, created by earthy, human, profane forces, and claims they are unalterable features of human existence. This philosophical error, that of confusing the man-made with the given, excuses man's role in creating the afflictions that torment him, a maneuver that denies a political consciousness space to exist, only to replace it with idle speculation about a metaphysical freedom that finds no handle in this man-made world.[8] Existentialism, then, far from being a radically liberatory philosophy, might be the ultimate insider trick.

As Marcuse insisted, existentialism as Sartre presents it, is "a morality which teaches men to abandon all utopian dreams and efforts and to arrange themselves on the firm ground of reality."[9] Marcuse thus suggests existentialism is a curious and irresponsible fatalism, an acceptance of this world's absurdity, which is not an ontological feature of the world, but a contingent, historical development brought about by man's actions and choices. Our existential anxiety should be a spur to investigation, political critique, and activism, not a quiescent acceptance of our material discomfort as a feature of existence.

To understand the force of Marcuse's critique, imagine an anxious middle-class person being told that his anxiety is "ontological," a signal of his freedom that he cannot espy in his limited job and economic prospects, as he is squeezed by mortgages, by college tuition fees and exorbitant medical bills. This will not reassure him when he considers the fate of his children in the battle place of the market, the cut-throat competition of admissions to prestigious colleges, or the brutal world of catastrophic financial and biological disasters that seem a feature of the twenty-first century. These fears stalked us as Covid-19 scourged our lands. They brought the most American of fears into our minds: death on a sidewalk, corpses walked over by indifferent bystanders, medical treatment reduced and denied for lack of insurance, eviction from homes, children forced to work as prostitutes, reduced to drug addiction and early death, sent to prison for crimes of desperation. In this world, the choice that existentialists spoke of is laughable; we want, we need, we demand security and predictability instead.

Marcuse suspects that being told that we should consider anxiety incurable and a golden road to self-discovery is an invitation to accept the world as it is, an invitation to political and moral quiescence. It would suit those in power to know that those they have made anxious and fearful through their political and social arrangements are content to wallow in their anxiety and not take any action to reform the material conditions that brought it about. But how can my anxiety be only mine when I am an incurably social animal, a product of society and its always-operative social forces? Can my anxiety be ameliorated without also a change to the world around me? Does it speak of bourgeois liberal privilege to be speaking of nurturing one's anxiety when most people are working dead-end jobs, a perennial source of anxiety for them and their families? Political action and activism, rather than solitary contemplation and meditation, is the right antidote for anxiety in this world.

Marcuse therefore resists "this proclamation of the absolute freedom of man," for "the scope and content of his liberty and the range of his 'choice'" is instead, "determined by his specific socio-historical situation."[10] So, man's "liberty is limited, and his choice is prescribed to such extent that their interpretation in the existentialist terms appears like mere mockery."[11] The choice, the freedom existentialists speak of, the ones that libertarians valorize when they suggest that a fired worker is free to find another employer, or negotiate another contract, or move to another state to find a new job: this all appears a cruel joke to the hamstrung worker who finds herself exhausted, marginalized, and anxious. Marcuse suggests instead that our freedom is always a qualified one, determined by the social structures and historical moments that enclose us and reveal our choices to us. A choice that is not visible is not a choice at all, and while we may be able to point out theoretical choices, we need realistic ones sensitive to our abilities and capacities and social situationing too.

In our modern world instead, even our supposedly liberatory systems of thought construct and sustain anxiety. For instance, note how libertarianism—supposedly a political philosophy of freedom and emancipation from governmental control, by insisting on our right, and indeed, our need, to make choices in all domains of human interest, even ones where we might want to bank on a social consensus of public goods and values— creates anxiety. The endless shopping for medical insurance from a "menu of options" of deductibles, copays, networks of providers, and the like is merely the latest laughable self-inflicted injury in this domain; rather than being able to count on the guaranteed security of health care when we are ill, without regards for our employment status or class or age, we are forced into endless shopping at times of ill health, again and again thrust into zones of decisional anxiety. Is this the space where we expect freedom will flourish?

We might then ask whether the psychotropic medications we are so furiously prescribing and consuming for the profusion of disorders we have named and diagnosed are treating the disorders we claim to have isolated or treating the particular social and cultural condition we find ourselves in, mitigating its effects to make them more bearable? Understood in this fashion, our many anxiety medications would appear more like our old friends alcohol and cannabis with which we enthusiastically seek to take the edge off as the day draws to a close. Or is psychiatric medication like Prozac, as psychiatrist Peter Kramer once suggested, merely a form of "cosmetic pharmacology,"[12] one that fixes those parts of us that are out of joint with the rest of the world? Perhaps my anxiety is like a snub nose that needs some trimming to make it fit better into the aesthetic demands of the social and cultural world I inhabit? Critical theorists like Marcuse would suggest we are taking medication because we are alienated and set adrift by capitalism; what would be needed instead is a reordering of society, a change in its values and perspectives, to be achieved by activism, legislation, and discourse, not by consuming medications. As Marcuse noted in *One-Dimensional Man*, if "care could be provided for the ill, the infirm, and the aged" then we would make "quantifiable . . . the possible reduction of anxiety, the possible freedom from fear."[13] Perhaps the powers that be prefer, as a social solution to "mental illness," medication to meditation or mediation, because a medicated citizenry can be a docile self-satisfied one, content to switch channels or browser tabs in their sedated states.

In the nineteenth century, Marxist theorizing offered a diagnosis of an acute psychological affliction in response to the ills of capitalist industrial society that had become visible in the years following the Industrial Revolution: alienation. In his *Economic-Philosophical Manuscripts* (1844) Karl Marx made severe notice of the *alienation of labor* thanks to man's continued existence in a capitalist system that commodifies relationships, which deprives the worker of a meaningful connection with either the products or the value of the work he produces. Instead, deprived of ownership in any sense of his work or labor, or of the time with which to commune with his fellow workers, the worker "becomes poorer, the more wealth he produces"[14] because "the worker is related to the product of his labor as to an alien object."[15] The means of production—the factory floor, the machines, and now, the file servers, the hard drives—are not owned by the worker, and he lacks meaningful control over the conditions and terms of his work; he cannot set a price on his labor, and neither can he share in the profits of the sold product. We might not live in a rapidly industrializing nineteenth-century England, the conditions of which inspired Marx's polemical pen, but we should take note that the modern worker has steadily lost workplace and union protections along with wage parity and is subject to greater levels of precarity than ever before, a fact realized with brutal, life-threatening force by the world's "essential" workforces in 2020–22.

The continuation of such disempowered states for the worker—whether blue collar or white, whether skilled or unskilled—is that "the more the worker expends himself in work, the more powerful becomes the world of objects."[16] The "world of objects" becoming "more powerful" entails a corresponding dehumanization of the worker. Thanks to this alienation of the worker, the very products he makes exist "independently" and stand "opposed to him as . . . an alien and hostile force."[17] Once alienated from his work, his labor, the products of his labor, man proceeds to an alienation from himself, his fellow man, and from nature, for his free and conscious activity has become mysteriously alienated. Ironically, the harder the worker works, the stranger he makes this world for himself and the more he, the agent of his own eviction, renders himself homeless.

The resonance here between Heidegger's "uncanny" and Marx's "alienation" is crucial: thanks to the way we have chosen to organize the world of labor and commerce, the world has become strange to us. What makes our constructed world especially uncanny is that it is furnished with objects we ourselves have constructed, through our own labor and ingenuity. In the Marxist conception of alienation, even Heidegger's *Das Man* is alienated, for he, too, finds himself outside the world of meanings constructed by those who wield economic power over him. If the world of artifacts was supposed to be our signature on existence, it is one written in a writing we cannot recognize as our own.

Marx's analysis generates two observations relevant to understanding the uncanny world we live in. First, the world of artifacts, the built environment, though made by humans, is imbued by an alien and hostile force. Here, the alienated suffer from interpersonal, intrapersonal, and existential isolation, each producing its own distinctive brand of anxiety, stemming from our realization of our isolation within our social spaces. We find ourselves lonely, separate, and helpless, stranded amid an omnipotent and malevolent world's depredations, unable to comprehend its workings. In our contemporary times, two implacable, impervious forces rule our lives: finance and technology, the underwriters of this modern world, neither of which is comprehensible nor controlled by us. Our movement through this world is through a strange land; its workings are hidden from us, and we cannot ask any more, for all is proprietary, hidden away from our prying eyes through a combination of legal mechanisms and social agreement.

Second, *we are alienated from life itself*—our work schedules leave us little time to build or sustain relationships with friends and family, who too are commodified, reduced to their economic particulars—and thus we are alienated from our fellow human beings and ourselves. The characteristic irony of modern urban life is the feeling of isolation in a teeming city; no one has time for sex, or the quality food and entertainments, which are left for tourists on vacation to enjoy; to merely meet a friend entails a long series of booking appointments for a "good time" to "get a coffee." We are adrift and disoriented, cast about in a world of strangers and strange things with no attention or affection to spare for us; these strange entities may become sources of threats and dangers to our psychic and material well-being. We work and work, and in the end, our grand exits from this world are marked by deathbed lamentations of wanting to have spent more time with those we love, of regretting our seduction by, our implication in, this brutal, alienating world.

So, our alienated labor results in our alienation from life, from ourselves, from our fellow humans. What does such alienation feel like? Like anxiety, for it is anxiety. When "man is alienated from other men,"[18] we perceive others as strangers, their workings incomprehensible, shrouded in mystery; we find our fellow human beings inaccessible, preoccupied with assessing their alienation from others. Alienation from our own bodies, from external nature, exacerbates this feeling; we feel disjointed from the bodies that house and sustain us, from the thoughts we entertain, from the most basic particulars of personal relationships. The alienated human feels an emptiness that it attempts to assuage by relentless consumption of this world's material offerings. This consumption—as the Buddha could have told you—does precisely nothing to address our root alienation, for the relentless accumulation of material goods, the hallmark of success in our society, cannot but engender anxiety as these transient goods offer testimony only to the passing away of all things.

Our alienation from ourselves, from society, is an acute sickness; it is a fundamental estrangement, a separation from oneself, from nature, from work, from the products of our work, from the most physically immediate material circumstances of our lives; it is a spiritual sundering, turning us into exiles in this home of ours, surrounded by those we formerly regarded as family and friends. We are in this physical, empirical reality that we can sense, feel, see, and touch and smell, but we are not of it; we find ourselves in Heidegger's "uncanny," surrounded by strangeness. Our awareness of this manufactured strangeness, constructed and sustained by the economically powerful, is our new anxiety. This alienation, this separation, bids us place trust and obedience in "new idols," which need not be divine; the national and the financial beckon us with their promises of safety, power, and deliverance, and their demands for allegiance.

As we have seen, existentialists like Kierkegaard, the later Sartre, Tillich, and of course, Nietzsche do acknowledge—to varying degrees—the determination of man by his sociohistorical situation. And our modern age has new grounds for anxiety: creeping fascism, climate change, environmental collapse, economic inequality, all exacerbated by a social media system that aims to sell us as products to its paying advertisers. These new concerns give our primeval anxiety new forms, connecting with our existential concerns in ways that make them signals of this age's anxiety. If we were unsure before, we are ever more so, bombarded with choices, manipulated by data algorithms, our children the prey of those who view them as consumers for their products. As anyone who has had to quit social media, seeking a "detox" or a "digital cleansing," will confirm, the more time we spend with our technological saviors, the more we need rescuing: we find ourselves perpetually envious, dissatisfied with the lives we live, anxious and uncertain and insecure about the choices we have made, keenly suffering anxieties of guilt and condemnation, suffering from a dreadful ennui that is the inevitable product of extended time spent online. Our cognitive dissonance about our decisions is enhanced and exacerbated by others' decisions, now visible for us to cluck over and make us regret ours.

To live with anxiety in such a world is a task considerably more challenging than simply facing up to it: it requires a fundamental reconfiguration of the ways in which we have chosen to organize our societies, a task taken on with considerable enthusiasm by the politically active, who find that praxis can deliver them from fear—while they act. And yet, despite this activism, we must learn to introspect, to look deeper into our anxieties and concrete fears to see what else may lurk within. Even as we engage in social and political activism to change our lot, we are not guaranteed success; we must continue to live in uncertainty and doubt and partial knowledge. Moreover, the materialist conception of anxiety does not clash with the centrality of death anxiety or fears of nothingness in existentialist treatments, for our economic anxieties invariably bottom out into those two forms; when we fear the loss of income, we are fearing our inability to withstand this world's insults without the protection of our monetary armor. Our philosophical concerns may be dismissed with an invocation of "economic realities": "We would not be anxious if we all made living incomes and had affordable housing and health care." But even those who live in comfortable homes, have good health insurance that makes $250-per-session psychiatrists affordable, and send their children to Ivy League colleges suffer terribly from anxiety. As the Buddha knew well, even if all material gains were to be secured, we would not be free of existential anxiety—even if we if we had made our lives more meaningful by making this world a better place for our children, and in so doing provided the best kind of role models and examples for them to help them live with their own distinctive anxieties.

Combating and confronting anxiety requires acceptance, activism, and contemplation, an acute blend of which might be the salutary recipe for living with it.

LIVING WITH ANXIETY

Anxiety shows us life is a (finite) cascade of fearful situations: we are cast adrift in a sea, in a raging storm, but are pulled into a boat, which must make it to land, where we find the terrors of hostile animals, which may be mastered, only to find a hostile galleon filled with bloodthirsty pirates bearing down on us. We are fearful and threatened; we find relief and are assured of new fears; this is our station in life, with anxiety our invariant, inescapable companion. This realized, we are partway toward living with anxiety: we must go toward it. This is a critical point of resonance with the foundations of cognitive behavioral therapy and acceptance-commitment therapy, modern psychotherapeutic techniques that emphasize sustained, continual exposure to our worst fears as the preferred path to learning to live with anxiety. Moreover, once we accept that anxiety is inevitable, we may spend less time fighting it and simply wait for the wave to wash over us; its very familiarity may be its own best antidote. We may compound the suffering of existence, "the first arrow," with anxiety about anxiety, the "second arrow"; but our original burden is quite enough. To understand we will always be anxiety ridden is to allow, too, for compassion and empathy for our fellow humans; we should especially find compassion in the face of anxieties impervious to life's circumstances: in the domain of the existential, the world's wealthiest and powerful suffer like we do; the material particulars of their lives are eased by their power and wealth, which cannot, though, relieve them of the fears of nothingness, death, the pain of the loss of loved ones, the terrors over the fate of their children, their worries about "incorrect" decisions. This lot of those supposedly more fortunate than us should reassure us about our assigned helpings of fortune too.

In acknowledging and accepting as inevitable, and living with, anxiety, we step a little closer to understanding who and what we are. If we are willing to sit with our anxiety, we may find it reflects our life's most important decisions, our most personal and deeply held commitments and values, the inflexion points at which inchoate moods crystallize into, and identify, concrete fears. Anxiety, as psychoanalysis informs us, is a message to us from the many bits that hold us together; we should listen to, and perhaps resolve, what our often-conflicting selves have to say to each other. If we find ourselves persisting in a task despite the accompanying anxiety, we have learned an important lesson about the valuation and importance of that task in our psychic hierarchies. And if being anxious is a form of knowing, then it enables us to do something, to accomplish something; it may make us write about our anxieties, or address an insecure relationship, or work on "improving" or "bettering" ourselves in whatever dimensions we find ourselves lacking, whether moral or intellectual. We should not, of course, expect our anxieties to remain the same as we, and our lives in tow, change; by paying close attention to their nature, their look and feel, we can track changes in ourselves and our "table of values." Anxiety is not singular; individual anxieties make up a sufferer's full complement. An anxiety may be a distinctive suite packaged for application to a particular situation of time, place, circumstance, and connotation. To know oneself is very often an injunction to know one's anxieties—individually, distinctively—and how they change and morph as we do, locked in a sympathetic dance of sorts.

As part of this navigation, we need to learn to recognize cultural and ideological triggers of our anxieties, to realize the damage done to our being by internalizing familial, social, and cultural advertisements of, or guilt-inducing admonishments to live, the "happy life."[1] The times of our lives are rarities, hopefully artfully and thoughtfully parceled out to our moral, familial, and intellectual commitments, but the cultural pressure on this time to perform is immense; every second must meet ideologically inflected, evaluative benchmarks for efficiency and consumption. The pressure for the perfect day—on vacation, at work, during leisure, during the week—grows; we see quite clearly—on social media—how our lives fall short of the supposedly ideal ones lived by our friends. A terror grows and festers within, shot through and through with a gnawing guilt: my life will not be the "best" (or even worth living); my work will not be the most fulfilling; my leisure time will not be the most rewarding; my children will not be the most precocious. My existential failure is foretold as these anxieties of guilt, and meaning, and purpose crowd our minds. Our life must acquire a certain number of (digital) approvals and endorsements to reassure us we have made the right choices. Anxiety is our response to the mythical requirement, the forbidding injunction in fact, that we must live according to normative standards drawn up for us, that this life and all its pleasures could be ours, if only we would do the "most essential," "the best," and not miss out on the "essential" or the "must-see." We seek instruction in what we must do; and if we do not do things the way guidebooks—religious or moral texts, or corporate brochures—tell us, then we will have missed out on the right life, the magnificent views others have curated and held out to us as attractions. There is some right slice, some right or best view of this existential panorama, which we must endeavor to obtain. We are persistently reminded the worst sin of all is to not have lived "the right life"; that we are wasting our lives if we do not let the aesthetic of efficient utilization guide our every step, our every foray. We have talents; we have limited time; all is possible; all could be ours: if only we lived the right way. We know the counterpoints to these oppressive nostrums, but we cannot internalize them; conformity and ideology beat us down. We have too many guides for the perplexed; perhaps we should be more suspicious, as Nietzsche urged us to be, of moral instructions and life plans that create us in a "bad conscience," saddling us with a guilt-stricken, anxious view of life; should we, perhaps, entertain uncertainty and the possibilities of the unlived life?

Our culturally entrenched norms, of course, promise us a path to happiness: the right education, the right job and material gratification, romance with the right partner, parenting kids who meet social standards of success and accomplishment, and so on. When we realize these conventional paths do not work, that the normative weight granted to prescriptions for life do not map on to the actual satisfaction to be attained from them, we develop an anomic relationship to this world, an acute, existential dissatisfaction with this world's arrangements and imperatives and the life they force on us. Our self-directive is to accept there is no required solution, no correct path, and to settle for a plurality of perspectives and "life solutions."[2] The great Chinese philosopher Zhuangzi, through his dazzling, often-nonsensical philosophical poetry, urges us to maintain just such an ironic distance from the demands of this world; we must learn to practice a kind of detached engagement with the ensnarement this world offers. Our humanity lies in the gap between our sense of who we are and our sense who we sense we might be; a distinctive shading and characteristic of this play of life is anxiety over whether we will lose our way in our journey across the divide. A pluralist approach to life can convince us that there was no path there to be lost, other than the one we made with our own steps, for even if we achieve culturally and socially recommended accomplishments, and meet prescribed milestones, anxiety sets up residence in our being. Our success does not protect us against anxiety; it merely gives us a different vantage point to experience it. The anxiety of the "successful" may be usefully contrasted with the anxiety of the still striving or the "failed," but it is anxiety, nonetheless.

What we call "life problems," or more fashionably, "life stressors," are, of course, manifestations of acute anxiety. We find existential anxiety wherever major or minor life events occur (indeed, as the existentialist sensibility promises us, there is not and cannot be any such thing as a "minor" decision): changing undergraduate majors, divorces, moving cross-country, changing jobs, getting vaccinated, choosing a career or vocation or life path. These decisions are invitations to anxiety; they force us to commit, to accept final decisions, which foreclose other options, paths, and escapes;[3] they force us to reckon with the tragic sense of life, that very often, we will confront dilemmas that will force us to irrevocably choose between two equally treasured values. This is especially true in the case of moral dilemmas, which when posed as puzzles might make us think there is a correct answer, waiting to be discovered or calculated by us. Unfortunately, there is not; you will get something "wrong" and be forced into an anxiety-ridden tragic corner.[4] Nothing, therefore, is more terrifying than a fork in the road: in both directions lie the fear of the unknown, the anguish of cognitive dissonance, of regret.

Our life's dilemmas, then, of which there is an endless supply, tempt us, ensnare us with fearful and ecstatic possibility. Like a perplexed and fearful Buridan's ass,[5] we vacillate endlessly and anxiously between the poles of choices, wallowing in stasis, in uncrystallized fears. Jorge Borges's "garden of forking paths"[6] is a veritable forest of anxiety as it confronts us with a profusion of choices, each partially visible and understood; here, there are too many possibilities, inducing in us a paralysis of freedom, especially when we sense we lack guidance, when we sense we cannot proceed without a map of each forking path. Because the future never ceases to be such a garden, our anxiety can never end; even as we head for our deathbeds, we, or our loved ones, will still have to make decisions: This medication or that? Continue treatment or discontinue? Quality of life or quantity of life? Should we spend the money on this expensive treatment or not? Who shall I favor in my will? Who shall I excommunicate as I die, making clear my displeasure at them as I depart into oblivion?

As an illustration of the centrality of anxiety to conventionally understood "life problems," consider the supposed "midlife crisis," an acute anxiety of meaning and responsibility visible in the questions it raises, which resonate with the taxonomy of anxieties posited by Tillich:[7] Is this all there is? Have I made "enough" of my life? Have I lived the "right" life? I made so many decisions; look at the pass they have brought me to; why did I not make others? Time is running out; which ones of my desires must I satisfy? The midlife crisis is, most profoundly, a species of anxiety about the life lived and not lived thus far, and the life yet to be lived. Prescriptions for resolving it are solutions for anxiety: we should engage in ongoing acts of creation and contemplation, in never-ending, "atelic" projects with no defined goals or end points such as playing guitar, as opposed to learning guitar to perform at Carnegie Hall; we should dedicate ourselves to social and larger causes, whose periods of resolution exceed our lifetimes; we should allow our creativity to flower through engagement with the wider world; we should enter into a sincere commitment to relationships with family and friends, treasuring the time we spend with them, recognizing it as *the existential good par excellence whose presence in our lives we should strive to maximize*; we should be good examples, even in the face of our fears, to those we love, for how to live and die.[8] If life is "a journey with destinations," we have anxiety about "arrival," about "the wrong destinations," about "failure to complete journeys," about "getting lost by taking the wrong forks"; but if there is "only travel, onward," we can sink back, fully cognizant that around the next bend may lie terrors yet unimagined. The so-called project or bucket-list life, as the Buddha might have warned, is characterized by signposts for failures; failure to achieve a project is cause for sorrow, guilt, and self-flagellation, while success in achieving one is merely occasion for ennui and doubt and the restless look for yet another project,[9] and for the anxiety arising from guilt over the list's still-incomplete status.

Can I "heal" myself of my anxiety without "losing" myself? This seemingly absurd question captures the instinctive sense we have that we, our selves, are complex physical, conceptual, and affective structures; a body, a set of beliefs, a complex of interrelated emotions; change your anxiety, and you change yourself; you cannot change one thing without changing everything else, for I "own" my anxiety, as part of my own distinctive personality and "style";[10] it animates my every step, my every resolution. Those who take psychiatric medication often find "parts" of their personality "gone missing," rendering them unrecognizable to their friends and sometimes to themselves; this mixed blessing may not be acceptable to all.[11] This anxiety, the one that has made me pursue philosophy, and hiking and climbing, which has made me reorder my life since my precious daughter was born, since I resolved to enter the commitment of a lifelong partnership with her mother: without it, I would not recognize myself. My anxiety renders my existence in this world, a distinctive and singular aspect; my anxiety is what makes my "being-in-the-world" what it uniquely is.

But if anxiety is a part of existence, and if we can never be free of it, then why not be merciful, and simply use psychiatric medication to end the pain? What gets lost in the prescription of medication for anxiety and other psychological disorders? The oldest antimedication claim of all is that taking it forecloses engagement with whatever issues are causing the anxiety—that it precludes the very introspection being touted in these pages. But a suggestion that we should "sit back and ride your anxiety out" can seem offensive and misdirected, not sensitive enough to the suffering experienced by those who do take medications or find their anxiety attacks the most terrifying experiences of their lives. I do not wish to trivialize the acute suffering of those who suffer from psychological anxiety disorders, to romanticize anxiety, to become a poet of anxiety, offering lyrical descriptions of painful pathologies from a safe vantage point. Still, even those who seek out medication and find relief will need to think through the existential anxiety that will remain and continue to underwrite the fears life's passages will create. Anxiety *is* the most plebian thing of all, the living breathing spirit of what it is to be human. We should treat it and live with it accordingly.

Sometimes, psychiatric medication might be needed to make working with anxiety tractable; sometimes medication can make it possible for us to work on "psychological problems" that have now acquired a clearer definition and outline. I have yet to hear of anyone though, who says that medication *cured* them of their anxiety, though it did make it more bearable, making them "functional" even if not "high achieving." An anxiety medication is "effective" if those taking it are not incapacitated and can perform those essential tasks—personal or professional—that require their attention and work. They have been reintegrated back into family and society, made functional again.

This very functionality of the medicated breeds suspicion, of course, that anxiety medications and their overprescription are part of a "get back to work" ideology unsympathetic to the genuine existentialist crisis of the worker, the parent, the child, the young adult striving to find their way forward in a confusing and disorienting world. Such medicated people are not anxiety-free: they will not stop worrying about their death or that of loved ones, or fearing the unknown, which may conceal all sorts of terrifying misfortunes. They will not be spared their dose of the suffering that arises in response to the very fact of existence, to the existential trifecta of existence in time, finiteness, and self-consciousness; and consequently, to the man-made world we have erected. Their anxiety has gone from being pathological to being the usual "quota" that every human being is allotted. We still need philosophical introspection to help us understand why the anxiety medication might have worked in some biologically primed cases and not in others, and why it cannot go any further in yet others. More to the point, just because we can alter our biological structure of thought does not mean that the *meaning* of our thoughts is lost. We still need philosophical reflection to help us understand and live with the quantum of anxiety sent our way by those thoughts.

There are costs to psychiatric medication too:[12] its often-prohibitive expenses; its many perplexing and often terrifying side effects; the difficult traumas of constantly drug switching visible in those patients of psychiatric medications who seem to be perpetually adjusting dosages and combinations and complaining about their effects wearing off; the varied long-term effects, which remain poorly understood and studied; and the acute problems of withdrawal. The very consumption of psychiatric medication induces a variant of anxious responses, sensitive to their promises: Is my medication working? Why do not I feel instantly better? Why has my medication's efficacy decreased? Am I without hope now that this magic chemical potion has failed to work? Will I ever be able to stop taking medication and just be a normal person? Must I keep the fact of my medication a secret from those who know and love me? Will I be considered weak for taking such medication? (The stages of life we experience do make a difference to the anxiety we experience and the remedies we seek out in response; the adolescent's anticipation of the life that lies ahead makes a significant difference to this experience, as does the middle-aged adult's anxiety over the life lived, and the pain and suffering of the advancing years yet to be lived. A supposed "quick-relief" medication might be thought to be more attractive to the latter, but as the United States' adolescent mental health crisis shows, such is not always the case.)

As things stand, our cultural overprescription of medication has changed the very definition of an "anxiety disorder"; it is now "that affliction for which you are prescribed antianxiety medication." Whatever the relationship of biochemical structures to mental health and illness, it is more complicated, and with considerably more room for cognitive interventions and psychosocial understandings, than our current psychiatric and medicalized fashions allow for. At the least, decisions about whether to medicate our anxiety should be more nuanced than they are in our culture. The intellectual and academic prominence of materialist models of the mind, which sustain medicalized notions of mental health dependent on rapid pharmaceutical intervention; our recurrent social embarrassment and anxiety when confronted with the "psychological problems" of those we love and care for; the cultural placement and entrenchment of pharmacological psychiatry; our pressing concerns to grease the wheels of industry with an available, efficient, productive work force: these factors ensure psychiatric medication is our most ready social and cultural response to anxiety. Many anxiety medications are, too, productivity enhancers; students at expensive private universities, corporate lawyers, investment bankers, tenure-seeking academics, day traders: all "pop ADHD meds" to pull off overnighters to get those precious grades, to meet onerous deadlines, to keep the registers clicking, the turnstiles whirring. But we sense our family, friends, and children are overmedicated, that the pressures of our culture and its economic predicaments leave us little time for self-understanding as we rush from work to family to child care to medical appointment; we are far from living the examined life, all the while finding our fundamental existential, moral, and spiritual anxieties remain as before. (On a related front, the new "psychedelic revolution" on both psychiatric and cultural fronts is fueled by a rising awareness of the potential of psychedelics to let its users break free of culturally imposed medical and material solutions to mental health problems.)

Importantly, if our desires induce guilt, and therefore make us anxious, for they are forbidden by our society, family, or workplace, then medicating our anxiety is a way for us to forswear these desires and seek respectability instead; when we are forced to repress our desires and engage in constant disguise to not be found out, we make ourselves candidates for anxiety. These desires are not exclusively sexual; they may, too, be indications of not wanting to be bound by preestablished normative claims on our lives: the self-exiled former member of a religious group or the corporate dropout is also acting on such a fundamental desire. The rejection of anxiety, the desire to not feel it, may be revelatory of a deeply felt, perhaps-even-more-anxious response; to medicate the anxiety may indicate a resistance Freud would suggest is underwritten by fear of finding out who we are, what desires we harbor, what grudges we bear, which guilts torment us. Smashing idols is never easy.

Thinking through our anxieties, then, may be politically and morally problematic; it may be unsettling and disruptive to our social and personal relationships. We may come to realize our culture and its advertisements for the "good life" have damaged us; that our social arrangements oppress and alienate us, rendering our personal lives hollow and harried; that our national and global politics is saturated with a malevolent rhetorical and actual violence; that for too long, we have been processing personal traumas by ourselves under the pressures of a toxic masculinity or a circumscribed femineity; that we have engaged in brutally self-destructive bouts of self-critique and hatred in response to the world's demands on us; that we live in lands where too many are turned into the homeless and mentally ill flotsam and jetsam who litter our urban spaces. Medication might numb us to these appalling realizations, not letting us feel a dread and resultant anger that has considerable political and moral valence. Our medicated states might be precisely the ones needed to keep us quiescent and amenable, and our social and political arrangements and their associated power relations of dominance and subjugation stable. Thinking about our anxiety may be the road to self-understanding *and* to comprehending the relationship the world and its arrangements has to us; it may then be a disruptive force, socially, morally, and culturally. The narcotizing, distracting, numbing effects of our social entertainments and responsibilities have long offered defense mechanisms against the corrosive anxieties of its members. But a repressed anxiety is expressed as neuroticism; our societies may be breeding neuroticism by not allowing their members to experience and understand their anxiety.

Perhaps anxiety—precisely because it affords self-discovery, reconceptualization, and self-construction, or provides opportunities for world-changing activism—should not be medicated out of existence. (The French philosopher Blaise Pascal noted long ago that people employed "diversions" to escape "thoughts of themselves.")[13] But what of pathological anxiety, the so-called generalized anxiety disorder, the panic attacks that physically incapacitate people, which leave many crippled and barely functional? Where is the boundary to be drawn between those species of anxiety and the kinds I have attempted to describe and interpret? From the perspectives presented in the previous pages, whether Buddhist, existential, or materialist, our various materially influenced anxieties are our maladaptive reactions to the existential concerns of death, nothingness, meaninglessness, and absurdity; *our material arrangements exacerbate our preexistent existential suffering*. From such a philosophical perspective, our distinctive psychopathologies result from the interactions of the conscious and unconscious defense mechanisms we have developed to help protect us against the trifecta of fundamental existential anxieties that Paul Tillich summarized so eloquently.[14] The existential anxiety described in the pages above *can* then underwrite complex psychological disorders, with their manifestations determined by individual physiology and psychosocial histories; we should consider the possibility, as touted by existential psychotherapists and philosophers and theologians, that existential anxiety, dukkha, and death anxiety are the foundation, the basement, of all named anxiety-related phobias and disorders. And so, medication may be necessary and desirable when our worldly anxieties become neurotic and crippling—a distinction present even in an existentialist philosopher like Kierkegaard—but it is an "illogical belief" that mental health consists in being anxiety-free.[15] At least one species of anxiety will persist; and as the Freudian and materialist theories of anxiety reassure us, so will others unless we radically change the world and our societies as well.

The Buddha considered the supposed eternal, immortal, unchanging self to be a dynamic bundle of ever-changing perceptions and thoughts and images; we are, too, a bundle of anxieties. By examining them—to see what vexes us, makes us anxious—we come to know who we are. Anxiety is a reminder that our selves are more diffuse and disorderly than we might imagine, that there are more bits to be seized as they swirl about and inside us. If our world "cannot be understood independently of the emotional reaction through which the world's nature is revealed,"[16] then the world we live in is shaded by our anxiety; *to learn to live with it is to change the nature of the world we inhabit.*

I am an anxious person; I respond with anxiety to this world's offerings. I am a better person for my knowledge of this state of affairs; by learning about my anxieties, I have gained an acute self-knowledge about my life, my passions, my commitments, my deepest fears. In writing about anxiety, then, I *must* indulge in autobiography. For instance, unsurprisingly, I experienced visceral anxiety while writing this book. I associate anxiety with writing and writing with anxiety; it informs my nervous return to the writing desk, the hurried stepping away from it, the persistent seeking of distraction online or elsewhere, the panicky procrastination on the production of a readable draft, my persistent dissatisfaction with what I write, my relentless self-castigation and self-doubt over the words I put down on paper. But anxiety about what I write informs me writing is valuable to me, that failure here means failure everywhere for me. Without my own peculiar anxiety, I would not be the writer I am; I would not be the father, the husband, the friend, the professor, the climber, the philosophical counselor I am.

The psychic burden of anxiety, then, may be offset by the gains in self-knowledge it affords; to experience anxiety is to experience our social self, with its attendant cultural and moral responsibilities, in the making. When we experience and work through the dissonance generated by anxiety provoking decisional forks of choice and relinquishment, the resultant conflict and self-examination can be acutely productive of such knowledge too. A living with the phenomenology and the felt experience of the anxiety, then, a conscious wallowing in and inspection of it, can enable an investigation of the self; anxiety, as Kierkegaard claimed, is a "school" for the self; and such sites of learning are frequently those of examination, of brutal testing of our limits. Because of my anxieties, I have come to understand why I am the philosopher I am, why I hold the views I do, why I do not trust that there is an inherent, essential, meaning or purpose to life, a final truth waiting to be discovered. My anxiety, an emotion and feeling, is intimately related to a hard-won knowledge about this world's eternally changing nature, one that often runs afoul of human plans or intentions or attachments or relationships. Why privilege some supposedly logical inference over this? Inferences and realizations are prompted by new inputs received, new beliefs formed, new inferences made; we may find ourselves forced toward the conclusion of a train of thought by anxiety, compelling us to move on till we face the truth of that which made us anxious.

My anxieties tell me I am still capable of feeling; they provide an acute reminder that I am alive and responsive, and yes, anxious. My anxieties about my family, my wife, my daughter, inform me that I have let myself become wrapped up in their selves; they inform me of the risibility of the claim that we are isolated beings whose boundaries terminate at our fingertips, at the surface of our skins; they inform me of what my self is. Thus does anxiety inform me of who I am.

Philosophy offers an expression of our deepest anxieties; it is stuck with the hardest questions, among them the ones that make us the most anxious, for in their asking, we pose the human constraints of their insolubility. If we found answers to these questions, we might not be human; we would be beings of another kind, for our current existential predicaments mark our being human. *To not be anxious would be inhuman,* for we would know all, we would have suffered no losses whose repetition we would fear, no final eventuality that would signal nothingness, no lack of time in which to make choices, back out on them, revise our commitments, and conduct corrections and do-overs. Without these metaphysical conditions realized, we remain afflicted by anxiety. Philosophizing, then, is an activity we perpetually engage in, just because we are always recovering from our incurable existential ailment, seeking not cures, but coping strategies for alleviating anxiety, by distraction, by doctrinal content, by introspection and self-examination, by immersion in love, and meaning-making activity.

Unsurprisingly, ancient contemplative philosophical traditions, Eastern and Western alike, offer us a pair of spiritual exercises common to all subsequently offered prescriptions for anxiety.[17] The first is "the theme of attention to the present instant,"[18] for "only the present is our happiness."[19] The wisdom of this injunction is apparent: it bids us turn away from the unspecified consequences and uncertainty of the future to face the current moment, an antidote to anxiety as we remain unconcerned with the unknown and unknowable. The similarity of this spiritual injunction to the suggestion that we occupy our time in this world with atelic projects should be immediately apparent. The concrete implementation of "being in the moment" is through committed practices of meditation and mindfulness, through a daily commitment to observing silence and contemplation of the world within, to learn how to not be identical with our emotions, but to become observers and cognizers of them, so that we may better manage them (empirical psychology terms this "metacognitive awareness").[20] This is a task that requires nontrivial discipline and commitment in the development and sustenance of a ritual for meditation, or in efforts to achieve "flow" in work and play, through meditative activities like running, hiking, climbing, playing music, making art, indulging in voluntary acts of charity, each of which encourages an outward, "unselfed" gaze removed from our normal selfish, self-centered preoccupations with reward, blame, self-aggrandizement, and guilt. When we meditate, allowing ourselves a first-person study of our consciousness, we allow ourselves to feel our anxieties; they rush into the mental spaces we leave open, reminding us of all that can go terribly, terribly wrong; they wash over us, almost making us leap out of our meditative postures. But there too, while meditating, we may inspect the nature of the beast; that it is a series of thoughts that can be inspected and let go. As the Buddha suggested, to meditate, to be mindful, is to understand how our mind works and how it creates the psychic world we inhabit. To do so is to work toward becoming masters of, and not hostages to, our minds.

The second spiritual exercise asks us to work on, via study and introspection, acquiring a vision of the world "from above," to rise "from individuality and particularity to universality and objectivity."[21] We are fond of colloquially referring to this as "taking the big picture in." I take this advice literally, as I seek out mountains and views and vantage points from where the world appears small, and I insignificant, and where I become aware of the eons of time that have passed, and will, while I pass on; this encounter with eternity is calming in distancing me from my usual self-centered preoccupations. More broadly, by turning our attention elsewhere, to the contemplation of beauty, to projects that are not ours, we can "unself" ourselves, take the focus off our own obsession with ourselves. Indeed, the more we focus on an external object or cause, the less we worry about ourselves; this is a virtuous self-forgetting, of turning to look at something else that is not us, to be so transfixed by its particularity and resultant beauty that our cares vanish. From such vantage viewpoints too, we acquire an understanding of the relationship of our lives to the rest of the various human and social assemblages and structures that enclose, sustain, and sometimes oppress us. From this elevated, lofty, and yet grounded perspective, we may notice we are not isolated in our islands of unhappiness and anxiety, an acute form of consolation productive of sympathy and empathy alike; importantly, we may notice that life has other fruits besides those of happiness, success, and worry-free states, namely, complexity, difficulty, and challenges. Here too, we may pay attention to the relationship our anxiety bears to other parts of ourselves; much like the artist might realize her creativity stems from her painful sensitivity to this world's offerings, we may come to realize the indispensability of our anxious states to those states we consider "productive" or "creative" or "emotionally sensitive," or best of all, "caring." (A mother's incurable and yet loving anxiety over the fate of her offspring presents itself as an exemplar.) This distinctive attention, one most acutely visible in that great literature and philosophy that is directed to particulars for the universal truths they convey, reminds us that anxiety is universal even as our own is distinctive. Paying "attention to the present and raising oneself to an objective view"[22] may thus, through self-knowledge and a cultivated empathy, bring about a mastery of "individual anxiety"[23]—especially if the present is anxiety itself. This elevated perspective suggests our lives are ongoing works in progress, with no suggestion we are incomplete or unfinished; this atelic thinking is an antidote for anxiety, for we forswear the angst and dread of the unattained normatively established goal. In understanding the ever-becoming nature of being, as the Buddha suggests, we do not expect what it cannot give; we do not disdain its blessings and carry around an impoverished, delusional vision of life, constructed out of the ideologies we have been instructed to devote our allegiances to.

Different philosophical approaches urge us to pay attention to varied aspects of ourselves to live with anxiety. Buddhist approaches urge on us forms of unselfing and the development of a universal compassion that places our miseries in acute perspective and allows us to make this world better for all; it urges on us a continual, disciplined facing-up-to and working-through of our worst fears; it urges us to become students, acute ones, of our own minds, to marry emotions with reasoned thought. Kierkegaard, Nietzsche, and Freud make us reflect on, and critically inspect, the social and moral norms that have generated guilt and shame and internalized repression (in seeking to emulate Kierkegaard and Nietzsche we risk the loss of social standing and status, a bargain we may be willing to make); Tillich and Heidegger make us fully and frankly acknowledge the basement of our fears, the animal terror of death that underwrites our every waking moment; Marcuse and Marx make us look suspiciously at the way we have constructed our world and its material arrangements. These relate to each other: our suspicions over the guilt induced in us by the world's normative and moral demands may make us respond with an activist energy and a defiant self-awareness that helps us live with our existential anxiety. My personal response to these philosophical guides has been to be cognizant of their fundamental insights, to return to their texts repeatedly, and to continue to integrate their claims into my conception of myself. A frank acknowledgment of the centrality of death anxiety to my life's passages has helped me accept it will be my constant companion, even as I am socially and morally emboldened by the defiance displayed by Kierkegaard and Nietzsche and empowered by the pungent critiques the materialist tradition offers. I have delivered myself to, and from, this world and its demands, a balancing act I will continue to work on till my dying day.

Too often, we resist our fundamental existential anxieties by insisting on the palliative fantasy of the Attentive King.[24] In ancient legends, kings rode through town to inspect their citizens, to gauge their happiness with their rule; as they rode through the streets of their capital, through throngs of their subjects, they would stop and call out to someone from the crowd they had chosen to recognize and reward; the lucky one was invited up and into the king's chariot, there to ride with him back to the royal palace, there to find his older life altered for the better. We are convinced we are the lucky ones; we have been picked out from the crowd; soon, the beckoning hand of the Attentive King will summon us to the royal palace. Mysteriously, we will escape the inevitable fate of human beings; this reassuring myth is untenable in the face of the constraints of existence. To wean our self from such facile consolations of deliverance—whether by earthly rescuers or divine intervention—is our primary existential responsibility and commitment, even if it entails confronting anxiety due to the reality of death or the inevitability of earthly misfortune. The existentialist response to the anxiety of our existential situation is engagement in the world, a "leap of faith" into the arms of a waiting God or the tasks of the world that need engagement and commitment—like activism to change this world's material circumstances, the ones that raise the chilling possibility that we might not even be able to put a roof over our heads, find the next meal, or clothe our naked bodies. An awareness of the obligatory and supererogatory duties we owe to others, to strangers, citizens, and friends, to the ones we love, should be all the motivation needed for us to spring into action and push back the anxiety of absurdity; meaning will not be gifted us; and we must make it with our acts and commitments. What better domain in which to exercise our metaphysical freedom than in the domain of political and personal action to fulfill our duties, to change our material circumstances and the tenor of our relationships?

Very often, we can be anxious because we lack the consolations of romantic or familial love; love promises blissful union, relief from terror, a place in this world, comfort when our end approaches, acceptance, and indeed, the most primeval of all consolations, that I will be taken in to a literal or figurative home, even as love acknowledges it cannot accompany us when we die and set off into the void. Freudian psychoanalysis has much to say about this desire to experience, again, a primeval "oceanic feeling"; anxiety is the feeling we experience when we are denied this comfort, when we dread a return to a time in our lives when that comfort was taken away from us. But besides seeking love, just as important is the injunction to *recognize the love that exists in our lives*; often we are lonely because we do not recognize the love we do receive, prompting a failure on our part to give. As Kierkegaard noted, "Would it not be sadder still . . . if love also should be only a curse because its demand could only make it evident that none of us is worth loving, instead of love's being recognized precisely by its loving enough to be able to find some lovableness in all of us?"[25]

Anxiety suggests our life is suffused with our courage, greater than that of a warrior of a martial epic. We stare unblinkingly at the ultimate disaster, the negation of ourselves, the loss of all we hold precious, which inevitably is our fate, and press on. We are used to considering ourselves cowardly; anxiety allows a self-portrayal that acknowledges a "hanging on in quiet desperation."[26] We exist in the face of disaster, our life a constant striving to maintain ourselves against external insult. The affect of this striving is anxiety, mastered only by the desire to move on, to reason, to create. As we continue to live at the edge of the unknown, anxiety informs us of the trajectories of lives we may live, the new self that awaits us as we move through our imperfect life. We will always be anxious; it informs us that we are human, and curious to find what we might yet be.

NOTES

Our Age(s) of Anxiety

1. Stossel, *My Age of Anxiety*, 52.
2. Freud, *Problem of Anxiety*, 23.
3. Annas, "Philosophical Therapy"; Cushman, *Therapeia*; Xenakis, *Epictetus: Philosopher-Therapist*; Mace, *Heart and Soul*.
4. I owe this choice of words to an anonymous reviewer of this book. This claim is made in extended form in my essay "Anxiety Isn't a Pathology."
5. Stossel, *My Age of Anxiety*, 52.
6. Beck and Emery, *Anxiety Disorders and Phobias*. The modern psychotherapeutic technique of "acceptance-commitment therapy" (ACT) is also inspired by Stoicism: Hayes, "Acceptance and Commitment Therapy."
7. Marguia and Diaz, "Philosophical Foundations of Cognitive Behavioral Therapy."
8. Van Dis et al., "Long-Term Outcomes of Cognitive Behavioral Therapy."
9. Cohen, "Philosophical Counseling."
10. Stossel, *My Age of Anxiety*, 36.
11. William Blake, "Grey Monk," https://romantic-circles.org/editions/poets/texts/greymonk.html, accessed May 2023.

Becoming and Being Anxious

1. Didion, *Year of Magical Thinking*, 4.
2. The Indian Buddhist monk and philosopher Nagarjuna is the foremost developer of this Buddhist doctrine; a full articulation can be found in the so-called Fundamental Verses of the Middle Way, reprinted in various Buddhist treatises. Garfield, Fundamental Wisdom, 293–321, provides a useful source plus accompanying commentary.
3. The following two pages draw from my essay "Of Therapy and Personal and Academic Anxieties."

4. May, *Meaning of Anxiety*, 189–90.

5. Freud and Breuer, *Studies in Hysteria*, 305.

6. "I'm Free," written by Mick Jagger and Keith Richards, from the Rolling Stones, *Out of Our Heads* (London Records, 1965). The song was covered by the Soup Dragons on their album *Lovegod* (Big Life, 1990).

7. Kierkegaard, *Concept of Anxiety*, 19n.

8. Marino, "Anxiety in *The Concept of Anxiety*," 312.

9. The term "ultimate concern" is attributable to Tillich, *Theology of Culture*, 6–7.

The Anxieties of Existence

1. Gowans, "Medical Analogies in Buddhist and Hellenistic Thought," 30.

2. Gowans, 30.

3. Introductions and more advanced treatments of the fundamentals of Buddhist doctrines may be found in the following sampling of a vast Buddhist literature: Gethin, *Foundations of Buddhism*; De Silva, *Introduction to Buddhist Psychology*; Siderits, *Empty Persons*; Hanh, *Heart of the Buddha's Teaching*; Fronsdal, *Dhammapada*; and Siderits, *Buddhism as Philosophy*.

4. Gowans, "Medical Analogies in Buddhist and Hellenistic Thought," 30.

5. Gowans, 30.

6. Gowans, 30.

7. Gowans, 30.

8. Robert Morrison convincingly argues this in his *Nietzsche and Buddhism*.

9. Siderits, *Buddhism as Philosophy*, 19.

10. James, *Varieties of Religious Experience*, 160.

11. Rhys, *Questions of King Milinda*, 40–45. The quoted excerpt here is a paraphrase of the full dialog.

12. Rahula, *What the Buddha Taught*, 30.

13. Rahula, 31.

14. This is a deep point of commonality with the ancient Greek philosophy of Stoicism.

15. There is a significant resonance with the existentialist tradition, which agrees that anxiety is to be approached, not retreated from.

16. This is a cornerstone of Stoic wisdom too. As found in Marcus Aurelius: "Never let the future disturb you. You will meet it, if you have to, with the same weapons of reason which today arm you against the present." Book 7, meditation 8, in *Meditations*, 106.

17. Chodron, *Comfortable with Uncertainty*, 1.

18. Chodron, 5.

19. Chodron, 7.
20. Chodron, 8.
21. Chodron, 23.
22. Chodron, 45.
23. Pollan, *How to Change Your Mind*.
24. There are important resonances here with the notion of *unselfing* attributable to Iris Murdoch, who notes, "The self, the place where we live, is a place of illusion." Murdoch, *Sovereignty of Good*, 91.

Free to Be Anxious

1. Ludwig Wittgenstein famously remarked, "A philosophical problem has the form: 'I don't know my way about'"; *Philosophical Investigations*, 123.
2. Morstein, "Anxiety and Depression."
3. Kaufmann, *Without Guilt and Justice*, 7–28. Existentialist thought is not, though, merely a nineteenth-century European phenomenon. It is temporally, spatially, and culturally diverse. By "existentialism" here, I do not exclusively mean that French movement associated with Jean-Paul Sartre and Simone Beauvoir but include too its theoretical forebearers, most prominently the trio of Kierkegaard, Nietzsche, and Heidegger.
4. The term "ultimate concern" as noted, is originally attributable to Paul Tillich, *Courage to Be*, 6–7; these concerns receive an extended treatment in Yalom, *Existential Psychotherapy*.
5. Kaufmann, *Without Guilt and Justice*.
6. Sartre, "The Humanism of Existentialism," in *Essays in Existentialism*, 36.
7. Sartre, 37.
8. Sartre, 41.
9. Sartre, "Freedom and Responsibility," in *Essays in Existentialism*, 68.
10. Morrison, *Nietzsche and Buddhism*.
11. This point is made most eloquently in the opening sections of *The Birth of Tragedy*. A good introduction to Nietzsche may be found in Kaufmann, *Nietzsche: Philosopher, Psychologist, Anti-Christ*. The classic works of Nietzsche most relevant here are *Human All Too Human*, *Beyond Good and Evil*, *Daybreak*, *Thus Spake Zarathustra*, *Twilight of the Idols*, and *On The Genealogy of Morals*; the best translations are those by R. J. Hollingdale and Walter Kaufmann. Newer highly regarded translations may be found in Cambridge University Press's editions of Nietzsche's major works.
12. Plato, *The Republic*, Thrasymachus speaking in 344c.
13. It is subject to varying readings in the Nietzschean corpus; the slave revolt described in *On the Genealogy of Morals* speaks to an inversion of values, carried out

by the weak, that replace those of the strong; in *Will to Power*, power is understood more narrowly as an independence from demands made on us, a self-overcoming forged by exposure to trial and tribulation, by the pursuit of great goals. The power of the "noble soul" as noted in *Beyond Good and Evil* resides in their independence from conventional demands of morality.

14. Nietzsche, "What Is Noble?," chapter 9 of *Beyond Good and Evil*.
15. Nietzsche, "Old and New Tables," section 56 of *Thus Spoke Zarathustra*.
16. Tillich, *Courage to Be*, 47.
17. Tillich, 106.
18. Nietzsche, *Birth of Tragedy*, section 5.
19. Nietzsche, "On the New Idol," in *Thus Spake Zarathustra*, 75–77.
20. This claim is developed in Nehamas, *Nietzsche: Life as Literature*.
21. Hollingdale, *Nietzsche*; Safranski, *Nietzsche: A Philosophical Biography*.
22. The following three paragraphs are drawn from Samir Chopra, "Nietzsche on the Relief of Mortality," https://samirchopra.com/2020/06/23/nietzsche-on-the-relief-of-mortality/.
23. Nietzsche, *Daybreak*, section 501.
24. Nietzsche, "The Prologue," in *Thus Spake Zarathustra*, 41–42.
25. Nietzsche, *Gay Science*, section 341.
26. Ernest Becker makes this claim eloquently in *The Denial of Death*.
27. Kierkegaard, *Concept of Anxiety*.
28. Carlisle, *Philosopher of the Heart*; Garff, *Søren Kierkegaard*.
29. "Angst" is characterized as "an affective state or mood . . . based in ontological structures of being human." Beabout, *Freedom and Its Misuses*, 7.
30. Beabout, 21 (citing Kierkegaard, vol. 1 of *Journals and Papers*, 100).
31. Beabout, *Freedom and Its Misuses*, 45.
32. Beabout, 47.
33. Beabout, 47.
34. Beabout, 48.
35. Beabout, 48.
36. Beabout, 18.
37. Beabout, 19.
38. Marino, "Anxiety in *The Concept of Anxiety*," 319; Beabout, *Freedom and Its Misuses*, 63.
39. Kierkegaard, *Christian Discourses*, 80.
40. Beabout, *Freedom and Its Misuses*, 22.
41. Kierkegaard, *Sickness unto Death*, chapter 2, 55.
42. Beabout, *Freedom and Its Misuses*, 46.
43. Beabout, 47.

44. May, *Meaning of Anxiety*, 44. This section draws extensively on May's discussion of Kierkegaard on pages 30–47.

45. Nehamas, *Nietzsche: Life as Literature*.

46. Kierkegaard, *Sickness unto Death*.

47. May, *Meaning of Anxiety*, 47.

48. Kierkegaard, *Concept of Anxiety*, 89.

49. May, *Meaning of Anxiety*, 56.

50. May, 58.

51. May, 59.

52. Kierkegaard, *Concept of Anxiety*, 145.

53. Kierkegaard, 146n.

54. May, *Meaning of Anxiety*, 63.

55. Kierkegaard, *Concept of Anxiety*, 189.

56. Kierkegaard, 189.

57. Kierkegaard, 189.

58. The preceding three paragraphs are drawn from Samir Chopra, "Kierkegaard on Being Educated by Possibility (and Anxiety)," https://samirchopra.com/2020/08/28/kierkegaard-on-being-educated-by-possibility-and-anxiety/. The discussion of the relationship between possibility and actuality is from Kierkegaard, *Concept of Anxiety*, 187–96.

59. Kierkegaard, *Concept of Anxiety*, 141.

60. Kierkegaard, 192.

61. Kierkegaard, 187.

62. Kierkegaard, *Sickness unto Death*, 39.

63. Beabout, *Freedom and Its Misuses*, 59.

64. Kierkegaard, *Concept of Anxiety*, 89.

65. Beabout, *Freedom and Its Misuses*, 62.

66. Beabout, 62.

67. May, *Meaning of Anxiety*, 45.

68. Kierkegaard, *Concept of Anxiety*, 194.

69. Kierkegaard, 52.

70. Tillich, *Courage to Be*, 12. The trial, sentencing, and death of Socrates is the subject of Plato's dialogs *Apology*, *Crito*, and *Phaedo*.

71. Tillich, *Courage to Be*, 34.

72. Tillich, 32.

73. Tillich, 37.

74. Tillich, 35.

75. Tillich, 37.

76. Tillich, 38.

77. Tillich, 38.

78. Section headed "Three Types of Anxiety" in the chapter "Being, Non-being, and Anxiety," in Tillich, *Courage to Be*, 38–53.

79. Tillich, 42.

80. Tillich, 165.

81. Tillich, 165.

82. Tillich, 42.

83. Tillich, 36: "In the anticipation of the threat originating in these things, it is not the negativity itself which they will bring upon the subject that is frightening but the anxiety about the possible implications of this negativity." Sartre puts it thus: "I distrust myself and my own reactions . . . the recruit who reports for active duty [is] afraid of death, but more often he is 'afraid of being afraid.'" From "The Problem of Nothingness," in *Being and Nothingness*, in Sartre, *Essays in Existentialism*, 120. To see what Sartre is getting at, consider that my fear of drowning is a fear of a specific event, but associated with it is a formless anxiety: my fear of the unknown fear I will feel when I start to drown.

84. William Shakespeare, *Hamlet*, act 3, scene 1.

85. The preceding three paragraphs draw on Samir Chopra, "Dreams of the 'Undiscovered Country,'" https://samirchopra.com/2014/07/21/dreams-of-the-undiscovered-country/.

86. Section 40 of Heidegger's magnum opus *Being and Time* (1927) contains an extended discussion of "angst"; a more accessible discussion is found in his essay "What Is Metaphysics?"

87. A good expository guide to Heidegger is necessary. Consult Dreyfus, *Being-in-the-World*, and Richardson, *Heidegger*, for starters. Simon Critchley offers a brief popular treatment in the *Guardian*, July 6, 2009, https://www.theguardian.com/commentisfree/belief/2009/jul/06/heidegger-philosophy-being.

88. Magrini, "Anxiety in Heidegger's *Being and Time*"; Whalen, "Anxiety, the Most Revelatory of Moods"; "Lyonhart, Being and Time-less Faith."

89. Bergo, "Evolution and Force."

90. This is Kierkegaard's description of the state of "despair" that we might find ourselves in were we to not acknowledge our existential responsibilities.

91. James, *Pragmatism*, 27.

92. Heidegger, *Being and Time*, 298.

93. Heidegger's claims resonate with those of Tillich, who suggested that the threat of nothingness, of being wiped out from existence without a trace, is so extreme that we may seek identification with "something transindividual"—a social grouping, a religious cult, a political ideology, a nationalism, a political party—that promises an extension and prolongation of our identity through "certitude . . .

supported by tradition and authority." Our civilization's structures, of course, provide such security, that of a "prison." Tillich goes further than Heidegger in locating a specific social pathology here, for this "escape from freedom" results in a "a fanatical self-assertiveness" and intolerance visible in the attacks of "disproportionate violence" on putative heretics. Tillich, *Courage to Be*, 46–47.

94. Yalom, 171.

Repression, Conflict, Memorable Trauma

1. Freud's *Problem of Anxiety* (originally published as *Inhibitions, Symptoms and Anxiety*, 1936) offers the most comprehensive working out of Freud's earlier and later theories of anxiety. This discussion is further reliant on Richard Wollheim's concise and succinct explanation of Freud's theories of anxiety in *Sigmund Freud*, 239–49. Clear introductions to psychoanalysis and psychoanalytic theory may be found in Freud's expository *Five Lectures on Psychoanalysis* and the more rigorous *Introductory Lectures on Psychoanalysis*.

2. Freud, *Problem of Anxiety*, 19.

3. Freud, *Standard Edition of the Complete Psychological Works*, 3:109, 114, 150–51, 268.

4. This point is made especially memorably in Freud's unsparingly pessimistic *fin de vie* work *Civilization and Its Discontents*.

5. Malcolm, *Psychoanalysis*.

6. Freud, *Problem of Anxiety*, 21–32.

7. Wollheim, *Sigmund Freud*, 241–45.

8. Freud, "The Finding of an Object," in *Three Essays on the Theory of Sexuality*, 222.

9. Freud, *Problem of Anxiety*, 119.

10. Freud, 75.

11. Freud, 119.

Anxiety and the Social

1. Tillich, *Courage to Be*, 62.

2. Tillich, 110.

3. Stossel, *My Age of Anxiety*, 303.

4. This remark has been attributed variously to both Thomas Edison and Theodore Roosevelt.

5. Fromm, *Escape from Freedom*.

6. This is perhaps Hobbes's most oft-quoted line, from the section "The Incommodities of Such a War" in chapter 8, "Of the Natural Condition of Mankind, as Concerning Their Felicity, and Misery," of his masterwork *Leviathan*.

7. Marcuse, "Existentialism," 311.

8. Marcuse, 311.

9. Marcuse, 336.

10. Marcuse, 320.

11. Marcuse, 320.

12. Kramer, *Listening to Prozac*.

13. Marcuse, *One-Dimensional Man*, 237.

14. Fromm, *Marx's Concept of Man*, 95; excerpts from *Manuscripts* are on pp. 93–109, and all subsequent references to Marx are from here.

15. Fromm, *Marx's Concept of Man*, 95–96.

16. Fromm, 96.

17. Fromm, 96.

18. Fromm, 103.

Living with Anxiety

1. This paragraph draws on Samir Chopra, "The Tyranny of the Tourism Poster," https://samirchopra.com/2012/01/06/the-tyranny-of-the-tourism-poster/.

2. Gunnarsson, "Philosopher as Pathogenic Agent, Patient and Therapist," 180. Gunnarson terms this an "ironist solution" to philosophical melancholy, drawing on Rorty, *Contingency, Irony, and Solidarity*.

3. Yalom, *Existential Psychotherapy*, 171.

4. This is an important domain of moral psychology, where literature focuses our mind on the real-life consequences of decisions better than does formal ethical theory; literary narratives force us to reckon, through the messy lives and fortunes of its characters, with the fact that whenever we attempt to answer the question of what we are to do, we are also reckoning with the insuperable puzzle of what kind of person we want to be.

5. This alleged medieval paradox of free will, attributable to Buridan, describes an ass, both hungry and thirsty, that dies of both hunger and thirst, stranded between hay and water, for it cannot rationally decide between the two options.

6. Borges, *Garden of Forking Paths*.

7. Section headed "Three Types of Anxiety" in the chapter "Being, Non-being, and Anxiety," in Tillich, *Courage to Be*, 38–53.

8. Setiya, *Midlife Crisis*.

9. Milgram, *John Stuart Mill and the Meaning of Life*.

10. "One thing is needful—to 'give style' to one's character." Nietzsche, *Gay Science*, section 290.

11. Kramer, *Listening to Prozac*.

12. Joanna Moncrieff is a prominent critic of psychiatric medication and a member of the Critical Psychiatry Network. Her works *The Myth of the Chemical Cure*, *A Straight-Talking Introduction to Psychiatric Drugs*, and *The Bitterest Pills* amount to a sustained, comprehensive critique of psychiatric medication.

13. Pascal, *Penseés*, chapter 8.

14. Section headed "Three Types of Anxiety" in the chapter "Being, Non-being, and Anxiety," in Tillich, *Courage to Be*, 38–53.

15. May, *Meaning of Anxiety*, xv.

16. Gunnarson, "Philosopher as Pathogenic Agent, Patient and Therapist," 183.

17. Ganeri, "Return to the Self"; Hadot, *Philosophy as a Way of Life*.

18. Hadot, 84.

19. Hadot, 217.

20. Teasdale et al., "Metacognitive Awareness."

21. Hadot, *Philosophy as a Way of Life*, 242.

22. Ganeri, "Return to the Self," 119.

23. Ganeri, 119.

24. Irvin Yalom terms this a belief in "a personal specialness and inviolability" a component of a "major alternative denial system: the belief in a personal ultimate rescuer." Yalom, *Existential Psychotherapy*, 129.

25. Kierkegaard, *Works of Love*, 56–57.

26. Pink Floyd, "Time," from *Dark Side of the Moon* (Harvest Records, 1973).

BIBLIOGRAPHY

Annas, Julia. "Philosophical Therapy, Ancient and Modern." In *Bioethics: Ancient Themes in Contemporary Issues*, edited by Mark G. Kuczewski and Ronald Polansky, 109–27. Cambridge, MA: MIT Press, 2000.

Aurelius, Marcus. *Meditations*. New York: Penguin Classics, 1964.

Beabout, Gregory. *Freedom and Its Misuses: Kierkegaard on Anxiety and Despair*. Milwaukee, WI: Marquette University Press, 1996.

Beck, A. T., and G. Emery. *Anxiety Disorders and Phobias: A Cognitive Perspective*. Cambridge: MA: Basic Books, 1985.

Becker, Ernest. *The Denial of Death*. New York: Free Press, 1997.

Bergo, Bettina. "Evolution and Force: Anxiety in Kierkegaard and Nietzsche." *Southern Journal of Philosophy* 41, no. 2 (Summer 2003): 143–68.

Borges, Jorge Louis. *The Garden of Forking Paths*. New York: Penguin Modern, 2018.

Carlisle, Clare. *Philosopher of the Heart: The Restless Life of Søren Kierkegaard*. New York: Farrar, Strauss and Giroux, 2020.

Chodron, Pema. *Comfortable with Uncertainty*. Boulder, CO: Shambhala, 2002.

Chopra, Samir. "Anxiety Isn't a Pathology. It Drives Us to Push Back the Unknown." *Psyche Magazine*, November 4, 2020. https://psyche.co/ideas/anxiety-isnt-a-pathology-it-drives-us-to-push-back-the-unknown.

———. "Of Therapy and Personal and Academic Anxieties." https://samirchopra.com/2015/02/27/of-therapy-and-personal-and-academic-anxieties/.

Cohen, Elliot D. "Philosophical Counseling: Some Roles of Critical Thinking." In *Essays in Philosophical Counseling*, edited by Ran Lahav and Maria Da Venza Tillmans, 121–32. New York: University Press of America, 1995.

Cushman, Robert Earl. *Therapeia: Plato's Conception of Philosophy*. New York: Routledge, 2001.

De Silva, Padmasiri. *An Introduction to Buddhist Psychology*. London: Palgrave Macmillan, 2005.

Didion, Joan. *The Year of Magical Thinking*. New York: Vintage, 2007.

Dreyfus, Hubert. *Being-in-the-World: A Commentary on Heidegger's "Being and Time," Division I*. Cambridge, MA: MIT Press, 1990.

Freud, Sigmund. *Civilization and Its Discontents*. New York: W. W. Norton, 1989.
———. *Five Lectures on Psychoanalysis*. New York: W. W. Norton, 1990.
———. *Introductory Lectures on Psychoanalysis*. New York: W. W. Norton, 1989.
———. *The Problem of Anxiety*. New York: W. W. Norton, 1963 (originally published as *Inhibitions, Symptoms and Anxiety*, 1936).
———. *Standard Edition of the Complete Psychological Works of Sigmund Freud*. Edited by James Strachey. 24 vols. London: Hogarth, 1994.
———. *Three Essays on the Theory of Sexuality*. Vol. 7 of *Standard Edition of the Complete Psychological Works of Sigmund Freud*, edited by James Strachey. London: Hogarth, 1994.
Freud, Sigmund, and Josef Breuer. *Studies in Hysteria*. 1895. New York: Penguin Classics, 2004.
Fromm, Erich. *Escape from Freedom*. New York: Holt Paperbacks, 1994.
———. *Marx's Concept of Man*. New York: Frederick Ungar, 1965.
Garfield Jay, trans. *The Fundamental Wisdom of the Middle Way: Nāgārjuna's Mūlamadhyamakakārikā*. New York: Oxford University Press, 1995.
Fronsdal, Gil. *The Dhammapada: A New Translation of the Buddhist Classic with Annotations*. Boulder, CO: Shambhala, 2006.
Ganeri, Jonardon. *The Concealed Art of The Soul: Theories of Self and Practices of Truth in Indian Ethics and Epistemology*. Oxford: Clarendon, 2007.
———. "A Return to the Self: Indians and Greeks on Life as Art and Philosophical Therapy." In "Philosophy as Therapeia," *Royal Institute of Philosophy Supplement* 66 (Cambridge: Cambridge University Press, 2010): 119–36.
Garff, Joakim. *Søren Kierkegaard: A Biography*. Princeton, NJ: Princeton University Press, 2007.
Gethin, Rupert. *The Foundations of Buddhism*. Oxford: Oxford University Press, 1998.
Golomb, Jacob, et al. *Nietzsche and Depth Psychology*. Albany: State University of New York Press, 1999.
Gowans, Christopher W. "Medical Analogies in Buddhist and Hellenistic Thought: Tranquility and Anger." In "Philosophy as Therapeia," *Royal Institute of Philosophy Supplement* 66 (Cambridge: Cambridge University Press, 2010): 11–33.
Gunnarson, Logi. "The Philosopher as Pathogenic Agent, Patient and Therapist: The Case of William James. In "Philosophy as Therapeia," *Royal Institute of Philosophy Supplement* 66 (Cambridge: Cambridge University Press, 2010): 165–86.
Hadot, Pierre. *Philosophy as a Way of Life: Spiritual Exercises from Socrates to Foucault*. Oxford: Blackwell, 1995.
Hanh, Thich Nhat. *The Heart of the Buddha's Teaching: Transforming Suffering into Peace, Joy, and Liberation*. New York: Harmony, 1999.

Hayes, S. C. "Acceptance and Commitment Therapy, Relational Frame Theory, and the Third Wave of Behavioral and Cognitive Therapies." *Behavior Therapy* 35, no. 4 (2004): 639–65.

Heidegger, Martin. *Being and Time*. 1927. New York: Harper and Row, 1962.

———. "What Is Metaphysics?" In *Basic Writings*, 89–110. Translated by David F. Krell. San Francisco: Harper ands Row, 1993.

Hollingdale, R. J. *Nietzsche: The Man and His Philosophy*. New York: Cambridge University Press, 2001.

Hutter, Horst. *Shaping the Future: Nietzsche's New Regime of the Soul and Its Ascetic Practices*. Lanham, MD. Lexington Books, 2006.

Hutter, Horst, and Eli Friedland, eds. *Nietzsche's Therapeutic Teaching for Individuals and Culture*. New York: Bloomsbury, 2013.

James, William. *Pragmatism*. New York: Dover, 1995.

———. *The Varieties of Religious Experience*. New York: Penguin, 1982.

Kaufmann, Walter. *Nietzsche: Philosopher, Psychologist, Anti-Christ*. Princeton, NJ: Princeton University Press, 2013.

———. *Without Guilt and Justice*. New York: Dell, 1975.

Kierkegaard, Søren. *Christian Discourses*. Princeton, NJ: Princeton University Press, 2009.

———. *Journals and Papers*. 7 Vols. Edited and translated by Howard and Edna Hong. Bloomington: Indiana University Press, 1967.

———. *The Concept of Anxiety: A Simple Psychologically Oriented Deliberation in View of the Dogmatic Problem of Hereditary Sin*. New York: W. W. Norton, 2014.

———. *The Sickness unto Death*. New York: Penguin Classics, 1989.

———. *Works of Love*. New York: Harper Perennial, 2009.

Kramer, Peter. *Listening to Prozac*. New York: Viking, 1993.

Kurth, Charlie. *The Anxious Mind: An Investigation into the Varieties and Virtues of Anxiety*. Cambridge, MA: MIT Press, 2018.

Lyonhart, Jonathan. "Being and Time-less Faith: Juxtaposing Heideggerian Anxiety and Religious Experience." *Open Theology*, 2020. https://doi.org/10.1515/opth-2020-0003. Accessed May 2023.

Mace, Chris, ed. *Heart and Soul: The Therapeutic Face of Philosophy*. London: Routledge, 1999.

Malcolm, Janet. *Psychoanalysis: The Impossible Profession*. New York: Vintage, 1982.

Magrini, James. "Anxiety in Heidegger's *Being and Time*: The Harbinger of Authenticity." *Philosophy Scholarship* 15 (2006). http://dc.cod.edu/philosophypub/150.

Marcuse, Herbert. "Existentialism: Remarks on Jean-Paul Sartre's *L'btre et le Neant*." *Philosophy and Phenomenological Research* 8, no. 3 (March 1948): 309–36.

———. *One-Dimensional Man: Studies in the Ideology of Advanced Industrial Society*. New York: Routledge Classics, 2002.

Marguia, Edward, and Kim Diaz. "The Philosophical Foundations of Cognitive Behavioral Therapy: Stoicism, Buddhism, Taoism, and Existentialism." *Journal of Evidence-Based Psychotherapies* 15, no. 1 (2015): 37–50.

Marino, Gordon. "Anxiety in *The Concept of Anxiety*." In *Cambridge Companion to Kierkegaard*, edited by Alastair Hannay and Gordon Marino, 308–28. New York: Cambridge University Press, 1998.

May, Rollo. *The Meaning of Anxiety*. New York: W. W. Norton, 2015.

Milgram, Elijah. *John Stuart Mill and the Meaning of Life*. New York: Oxford University Press, 2019.

Moncrieff, Joanna. *The Bitterest Pills: The Troubling Story of Antipsychotic Drugs*. New York: Palgrave, 2013.

———. *The Myth of the Chemical Cure: A Critique of Psychiatric Drug Treatment*. New York: Palgrave, 2008.

———. *A Straight-Talking Introduction to Psychiatric Drugs*. Monmouth: PCCS Books, 2009.

Morrison, Robert. *Nietzsche and Buddhism: A Study in Nihilism and Ironic Affinities*. New York: Oxford University Press, 1997.

Morstein, Petra. "Anxiety and Depression: A Philosophical Investigation." *Radical Psychology* 1 (Summer 1999): 1.

Murdoch, Iris. *The Sovereignty of Good*. London: Routledge, 2013.

Nehamas, Alexander. *Nietzsche: Life as Literature*. Cambridge, MA: Harvard University Press, 1985.

Nietzsche, Friedrich. *Beyond Good and Evil*. New York: Penguin, 1973.

———. *The Birth of Tragedy*. In *"The Birth of Tragedy" and "The Case of Wagner."* New York: Vintage, 1967.

———. *Daybreak: Thoughts on the Prejudices of Morality*. New York: Cambridge University Press, 1997.

———. *The Gay Science*. New York: Cambridge University Press, 2001.

———. *"On the Genealogy of Morals" and "Ecce Homo."* New York: Vintage, 1989.

———. *Human, All Too Human: A Book for Free Spirits*. New York: Cambridge University Press, 1990.

———. *Thus Spake Zarathustra: A Book for Everyone and No One*. New York: Penguin Classics, 1961.

———. *The Twilight of the Idols and the Anti-Christ: or How to Philosophize with a Hammer*. New York: Penguin Classics, 1990.

———. *Will to Power*. New York: Vintage, 1968.

Pascal, Blaise. *Penseés*. New York: Penguin Classics, 1995.

Peterman, J. F. *Philosophy as Therapy: An Interpretation and Defense of Wittgenstein's Later Philosophical Project*. Albany: State University of New York Press, 1992.

Pollan, Michael. *How to Change Your Mind: What the New Science of Psychedelics Teaches Us about Consciousness, Dying, Addiction, Depression, and Transcendence*. New York: Penguin, 2019.

Rahula, Walpola. *What the Buddha Taught*. Dehiwala: Buddhist Cultural Centre, 1996.

Rhys David, T. W., trans. *The Questions of King Milinda*. Vol. 25 of *The Sacred Books of the East*. Oxford: Clarendon/Oxford, 1890.

Richardson, John. *Heidegger*. New York: Routledge, 2012.

Rorty, Richard. *Contingency, Irony, and Solidarity*. Cambridge: Cambridge University Press, 1985.

Safranski, Rudiger. *Nietzsche: A Philosophical Biography*. New York: W. W. Norton, 2001.

Sartre, Jean-Paul. *Essays in Existentialism*. New York: Citadel, 2002.

Setiya, Kieran. *Midlife Crisis: A Philosophical Guide*. Princeton, NJ: Princeton University Press, 2018.

Siderits, Mark. *Buddhism as Philosophy: An Introduction*. Cambridge: Ashgate, 2007.

———. *Empty Persons: Personal Identity and Buddhist Philosophy*. Aldershot: Ashgate, 2003.

Sorabji, Richard. *Emotion and Peace of Mind: From Stoic Agitation to Christian Temptation*. Oxford: Clarendon, 2002.

Stossel, Scott. *My Age of Anxiety: Fear, Hope, Dread, and the Search for Peace of Mind*. New York: Vintage, 2015.

Teasdale, J., R. Moore, H. Hayhurst, M. Pope, S. Williams, and Z. Segal. "Metacognitive Awareness and Prevention of Relapse in Depression: Empirical Evidence." *Journal of Consulting and Clinical Psychology* 70, no. 2 (2002): 275–87.

Tillich, Paul. *The Courage to Be*. 1952. 3rd ed. New Haven, CT: Yale University Press, 2014.

———. *Theology of Culture*. London: Oxford University Press, 1964.

Ure, Michael. *Nietzsche's Therapy: Self Cultivation in the Middle Works*. Lanham, MD: Lexington Books, 2008.

van Dis, Eva A. M., Suzanne C. van Veen, and Muriel A. Hagenaars. "Long-Term Outcomes of Cognitive Behavioral Therapy for Anxiety-Related Disorders: A Systematic Review and Meta-analysis." *JAMA Psychiatry* 77, no. 3 (March 1, 2020): 265–73.

Whalen, John T. "Anxiety, the Most Revelatory of Moods." *Akadimia Filosofia* 1, no. 1 (2015): art. 8.

Wittgenstein, Ludwig. *Philosophical Investigations*. 4th ed. Edited and translated by P.M.S. Hacker and Joachim Schulte. Oxford: Wiley-Blackwell, 2009.
Wollheim, Richard. *Sigmund Freud*. Cambridge: Cambridge University Press, 1981.
Xenakis, Iason. *Epictetus: Philosopher-Therapist*. The Hague: Nijhoff, 1969.
Yalom, Irvin. *Existential Psychotherapy*. New York: Basic Books, 1980.

INDEX

abandonment, 119
activism, 141, 155, 163
Adam, 73
agoraphobia, 114
alcohol, 26–27
alienation, 136–40
analytical philosophy, 30
antidepressants, 122
anxiety: acceptance of, 93; ages of, 1–2, 3; benefits of, 144; causes of, 8, 37, 48, 52, 87, 140; challenges regarding, 37; as crisis of meaning, 97–98; curing of, 9; defined, 2; disorders, 84, 128–29, 152; diversity of, 3; effects of, 20, 22; as essential, 95–96; existential, 42, 86, 147, 155–56; familiarity of, 143; as febrile and fertile, 23–24; forms of, 89; as human condition aspect, 12–13; as informant, 104; living with, 50, 141; manifestations/expressions of, 1; message from, 144; mood of, 87–88, 94–107; as the next day, 74–75; overview of, 2–3, 7, 9; persistence of, 1; as perspective, 20; philosophy as resource for, 5–6; psychic burden of, 157; as punishment, 127; reconceptualization of, 9–10; resolving, 109–10; as suite package, 144–45; terms regarding, 13; thinking through, 154–55; translations of, 53; triggers of, 145; types of, 13, 22; as universal condition, 3; valorization of, 128; welcoming of, 53, 58
Attentive King, 162–63
Aurelius, Marcus, 166n16
awakening, 38–39
awareness, 43, 68–69, 87, 88–89, 101

birth, 116–17, 118–19, 125–26
Borges, Jorge, 148
bucket-list life, 149
Buddha/Buddhism: approaches from, 161–62; codependent arising of, 19–20; doctrines of, 35; enlightenment from, 37; expression of, 52; Four Noble Truths from, 37–38; as the Great Physician, 35; overview of, 8; teachings of, 36, 49; Western view of, 38

Camus, Albert, 30, 105
cancer, 16–18, 27–28
capitalism, 136–38
Catholicism, 83
certainty, death of, 60–71
children, 51, 116–17, 119, 129
Chodron, Pema, 50
Christian existentialism, 59
Christianity, immortality doctrine in, 67

class anxiety, 129
climate change, 4
codependent arising, 19–20
cognitive behavioral therapy, 12
compassion, 161
The Concept of Anxiety (Kierkegaard), 71–85
conflict, 76–77, 78, 109–10, 113–14
consciousness, 77–78, 86, 88, 104, 146
cosmetic pharmacology, 136
courage, 81, 83–84, 85–90, 93–94
The Courage to Be (Tillich), 85–90
Covid-19 pandemic, 131, 132, 134
creativity, 80–81
cynicism, 131

Das Man ("everyman"), 96, 103, 132, 138
death: acceptance of, 91, 93, 104; anxiety of, 93, 162; awareness of, 87; of certainty, 60–71; fact of, 95, 97; fear of, 90, 91; fleeing of, 103; forms of, 125; freedom and, 28; lessons from, 26, 29, 32; personal stories regarding, 16–19, 23, 27–28, 32; trauma from, 26–27; as ultimate concern, 54; uncertainty of, 91, 103
decisional anxiety, 135
defense mechanisms, 105
deficit of attention, 24
developmental stages, anxiety and loss in, 116–17, 120
Diagnostic and Statistical Manual of Mental Disorders (DSM), 13
Didion, Joan, 19
discipline, 161
Dostoyevsky, Fyodor, 30
dread, 19, 28
dukkha, 35–36, 38, 40, 42, 43, 75

economic anxiety, 126, 127, 129, 132, 133–34, 141
Economic-Philosophical Manuscripts (Marx), 136–37
ego, 111
Eight-Fold Path, 38–39
emotions, 54, 70–71, 161–62. *See also* moods
existential anxiety, 42, 86, 147, 155–56
existentialism: Christian, 59; criticism of, 132–33; defined, 30–31, 167n3; overview of, 30–31, 53–54; relief from, 32; of Sartre, 56–57, 59–60; ultimate concerns of, 54; world engagement and, 163

faith, 59, 71–85, 82
the fall, 73
fatalism, 133
fate, 61–62
fear: anxiety and, 75; causes of, 124–25, 126; courage for, 81, 83–84; of death, 90, 91; displacement of, 114; example of, 100; of nothingness, 93; overview of, 73–74
forking paths analogy, 148
Four Noble Truths, 37–39, 52
fragility, of happiness, 43
freedom: anxiety and, 55–56, 76, 80, 128; as blessing, 71; burden of, 71; challenges of, 56; craving of, 78; dissonance regarding, 78–79; escape from, 171n93; limitations of, 134–35; overview of, 55; possession of, 58; shrinking from, 78; as ultimate concern, 54
Freud, Sigmund: on anxiety, 108–9, 111–15, 118–19, 126; on birth, 116–17, 118–19; on conflict, 110; on ego, 111; on helplessness, 118; on loss, 117–19; mature theory of anxiety of, 118; on

neurotic anxiety, 113–14, 117; psychoanalytic theory of, 8–9; quote of, 117; on reflection, 162; on repression, 112–13; on separation anxiety, 120–21; on sexual repression, 114–16; toxic theory of the libido and, 111–12; viewpoint of, 25

future, uncertainty regarding, 55

generalized anxiety disorder, 13–14, 155
God, 18–19, 61, 64, 68, 73, 125
Great Depression, 127
guilt, 79, 84–85, 145, 146, 162

hammer analogy, 101
happiness, 43, 146, 159
heart attack, 16, 27
Heidegger, Martin, 56, 71, 94–107, 162
helplessness, 118
Hinduism, 83
homosexuality, 122
human beings: as artists, 77; consciousness of, 77–78; creativity of, 80–81; defense mechanisms of, 105; as ethical individuals, 80; fragility of, 96; historical nexus of, 83; inauthenticity of, 96–97; internal psychic conflicts of, 78; limitations of, 87–88, 103; polarities of, 75–76; responsibilities of, 103; self-creation of, 76–77
Hume, David, 51

immigration, 126
immortality, 67, 68, 90, 92
impatience, 75
incels, 115
Industrial Revolution, 125
inquiry, as anxiety response, 5–6
Institute for Contemporary Psychotherapy, 21

intellectual virtue theory, 12
isolation, 73, 139

James, William, 41, 102
jealousy, 24
Jesus Christ, 82
Judaism, 83

Kierkegaard, Søren: on anxiety, 71–74, 76, 79, 82, 83–85; *The Concept of Anxiety*, 71–85; on ethical individuals, 80; as existentialist, 30; on faith, 59, 82; influence of, 56; on man, 75; overview of, 72; on psychic conflicts, 78; quote of, 31, 164; on reflection, 162; writings of, 72
knowledge, 42, 76
Kramer, Peter, 136

labor, alienation of, 136–38
libertarianism, 135
libido, 111–12, 117, 122
loss, 117–19, 120–21
love, 163–64

make-believe, 62
male anxiety, 126
Marcuse, Herbert, 9, 69, 132–33, 134–35, 136, 162
Marx, Karl, 9, 69, 136–40, 162
materialist alienation, 9
meaninglessness, of life, 31–32, 65, 106
medical insurance, 135
medication: benefits of, 150–51, 154; decisions regarding, 153; detriments of, 149–50, 152; function of, 135–36; limitations of, 44; overprescription of, 151, 152; as productivity enhancers, 153; promises of, 131; repression through, 153–54

meditation, 49, 159–60
mental illness, 128–29, 136
midlife crisis, 148–49
migration, 25
Milinda (Indian king), 46–47
mind, awareness and function of, 48–49
mindfulness, 49
misogyny, 115
modern age, 125
modern philosophy, 30
monogamy, 115
moods, 94–107. *See also* emotions
morality, 63
moral psychology, 172n4
mortality, 4, 67, 68–69

Nagarjuna, 165n2
Nàgasena (Buddhist monk), 46–47
Nausea (Sartre), 56, 99
neuroses/neurotic anxiety, 113–14, 117
Nietzsche, Friedrich: on anxiety, 61–62, 64, 65, 69, 84–85; characteristics of, 66; death of, 71; doctrines of, 67; on emotions, 70–71; as existentialist, 30; on the good life, 70; on immortality, 68; legacy of, 71; on morality, 63–64; on power, 63; predictions of, 66; on reflection, 162; writings of, 61, 69–70
nirvana, 49
No Exit (Sartre), 56
nonexistence, 88–90
normal, reconfiguration of, 127
nothingness, 57, 88–90, 93, 95, 97, 125, 170n93

The Outsider (Wright), 105–6

parents, 119, 126, 129–30
Pascal, Blaise, 155

pathological anxiety, 155
philosophical method, 12
philosophical reflection, 151
philosophy: as anxiety resource, 5–6, 158; benefits of, 32–33, 35; as form of therapy, 14; forms of, 30; function of, 158–59; importance of, to psychotherapeutic modalities, 11–12; living and, 31; overview of, 33–34; psychology and, 54; spiritual exercises from, 159
phobias, 114. *See also* fear
pluralist life approach, 147
politics, 131
Pollan, Michael, 51
pornography, 115
power, 63, 144
present, attention to, 159, 161
procrastination, 83–84
productivity, 153
project life, 149
Prozac, 21, 136
psychedelic revolution, 153
psychoanalysis, 110–11
psychoanalytic theoretical apparatus, 108–9
psychoanalytic theory, 8–9, 11
psychology, 54
psychopathologies, 109
psychotherapy, 20–22, 25, 29–30
psychotropic medications, 135–36

reaction anxiety, 116
reason, emotions and, 54
rebellion, 78
reconciliation, 110
reflection, 151
religion, function of, 60–61
repression, 112–13, 114–16, 121, 153–54

Sartre, Jean-Paul, 30, 56–57, 59–60, 71, 99, 133, 170n83
Schopenhauer, Arthur, 43
science, 31
self ("I"): anxiety regarding, 44; attachment to, 45, 47–48; dynamic bundles of, 44–45; as eternal, 45–46; existence of, 56–57; freedom and, 58; nothingness of, 51–52; stability of, 58
self-acceptance, 61
self-creation, 76–77
self-discovery, 134
self-dissolution, 102
self-knowledge, 109, 157
separation anxiety, 120–21
sexuality, 112, 114–16, 122
sin, 73, 74, 79
skillful balanced walking, 39
social media, 115, 140–41, 145
society/social anxiety: causes of, 129–30; freedom in, 135; medication and, 135–36; nonconformance with, 132; overview of, 121–22; pressures of, 132, 145; promises from, 146
spiritual deliverance, 71–85
spiritual exercises, 159
states of mind, achieving, 36
status anxiety, 129
The Stranger (Camus), 105
success, 147
suffering: causes of, 38, 40–41, 43, 52; Eight-Fold Path and, 38–39; ignorance and, 51; as life condition, 50–51; moralizing of, 63; overview of, 38; transformation and, 42–43
swimming analogy, 79–80

taking the big picture in, 160–61
technology, 4, 130–31, 140–41
temptation, of sin, 74

therapy, purpose of, 25
thrownness, 95, 100–101
Tillich, Paul: on anxiety, 85–90, 92–94, 126–27; *The Courage to Be*, 85–90; on faith, 59; on fear, 162; on freedom, 71; on meaninglessness, 65; quote of, 126–27
toxic theory of the libido, 111–12
tranquility, 36–37
transindividual, identification with, 170n93
trauma, 116–17, 118–19, 152
A Treatise of Numan Nature (Hume), 51
triggers, of anxiety, 145

Unamuno, Miguel, 30
uncanniness, 97, 99, 138, 140
uncertainty, 64, 74–75, 91
upward mobility, 3–4, 127

wealth, 144
white anxiety, 126
world: as abnormal, 96; acceptance of, 110–11; actions and choices within, 62; alienation and, 138; anxiety and, 48, 156; breaking down of, 98–99; characteristics of, 42; conditioning by, 100–101; consumption of, 139; demands of, 162; detachment from, 146; diversions of, 77, 105; emotional reactions to, 38; engagement with, 163; foundations of, 99; function of, 36; human beings' role within, 103; illusion of, 51; limitations of, 80; losses from, 109, 120; polarities of, 102; responsibility of, 57; uncanniness of, 138; vision from above of, 160–61
Wright, Richard, 105–6
writing, anxiety and, 157

Zhuangzi, 146

A NOTE ON THE TYPE

This book has been composed in Arno, an Old-style serif typeface in the classic Venetian tradition, designed by Robert Slimbach at Adobe.

GPSR Authorized Representative: Easy Access System Europe - Mustamäe tee 50, 10621 Tallinn, Estonia, gpsr.requests@easproject.com

www.ingramcontent.com/pod-product-compliance
Lightning Source LLC
Jackson TN
JSHW032355180925
91109JS00002B/1